The Sluggers

John Holway
Contributing Editor

and the Editors
of Redefinition

A
BOOK

The Sluggers

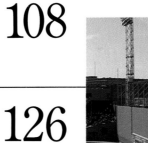

You funnel through the gate and wind your way through the cool concrete darkness of the concourse. Finding your section, you cross the narrow catwalk toward the bright window of green and blue ahead. Emerging from the darkness, your senses waken to the sound of ball against bat and glove, the landscape of seats, sky, and grass that's impossibly green. Suddenly, it doesn't matter what teams are on the field. What matters is the game they're playing.

A Great Day at the Plate

There are some stadiums where, on any given day, baseball's balance of power can be rudely disrupted. Pitching may be 75 percent of the game, but hitting is its most emphatic quarter, and in stadiums like Chicago's Wrigley Field, Detroit's Tiger Stadium, and Boston's Fenway Park, there are days that the hitters just take over. In Chicago, May 17, 1979 was one such day.

It was less a game than it was a relay race with bats. Hitting can be contagious, and when games start off as this one did, with 13 runs in the first inning, hitters grab the chance to fatten their stats and rough up pitchers. "The first thing you do after a game like this," said Phillie reliever Ron Reed, "is see if you have any broken bones." But not only Reed's earned-run average was fractured—his went from 0.43 to 2.55; Willie Hernandez' leaped from 2.87 to 5.50. Mike Schmidt and Dave Kingman, the National League's premier sluggers that year, led an unprecedented parade of power, as 11 balls cleared the ivy in the Phils' 23–22, ten-inning win. Kingman hit the most—three for Chicago; Philadelphia's Schmidt the first and last. In the four hours between Schmidt's homers, runs came in violent bursts. The teams combined for 50 hits, 24 of them for extra bases.

It was a familiar script for the Phillies and Cubs, who have used Wrigley Field as the stage for several memorable slugfests. In 1922 they set a standard that even the 1979 game couldn't meet, as the Cubs scored ten in the second and 14 in the fourth and hung on to win, 26–23. In 1976 Schmidt homered in four consecutive at-bats to lead the Phillies to an 18–16 win.

"Everything that was thrown up there was hit somewhere, by everybody," said Philadelphia Phils third baseman Mike Schmidt (opposite). In this 45-run slugfest against the Chicago Cubs, Schmidt hit the first and last of the game's 11 home runs.

As the game wore on, Phillies first baseman Pete Rose just got dirtier and more frustrated. The dirt came from the basepaths, the frustration from the Cubs' comeback.

Chicago first baseman Bill Buckner's grand slam came in the fifth and cut the Phillies' lead to 21–14. Chicago was back in the game!

The National League was full of sluggers in 1979. Kingman, Schmidt, Dave Winfield, Dave Parker, and George Foster were still in their prime, while Dale Murphy, Jack Clark, Andre Dawson, Larry Parrish, and Bob Horner stood as the next generation.

Six weeks into the season the Phillies came into Chicago in first place and playing .700 baseball. Pete Rose was leading the league in hitting, Schmidt in homers and RBI. The Cubs were in fourth, square at .500. And when his first-inning pop fly literally blew into the left field bleachers, Schmidt knew it would be a hitter's day. Schmidt owned Wrigley Field, having hit 21 of his first 204 homers there, but on this day the grand old park belonged to anyone with a bat in his hand. Cub starter Dennis Lamp was getting his pitches up, a disaster in a Wrigley wind, and Bob Boone's three-run shot knocked him out of the game. Then reliever Randy Lerch, who pounded two homers in the Phillies' 1978 division-clinching win over the Pirates, stroked a knee-high fastball from Donnie Moore into the second row of the left center field bleachers. When the wind blows from the south at Wrigley and pitchers hit opposite-field home runs, all order is banished from the game.

The 17 mile per hour wind not only blew a few balls out, it gave hitters enough confidence to tip the balance in their favor. "When the fences are so reachable, it makes everybody a better hitter," Schmidt said. "Every hitter becomes more relaxed, so he's less susceptible to good pitches. When everybody's banging the ball around like that, no pitcher looks good."

Kingman—who swung for the fences with perhaps the greatest singularity of purpose of any player—had watched as the wind blew Schmidt's fly over his head and came to the plate with two on in the first as if sitting down to Thanks-

The game was a writer's delight, spawning such journalistic flights as "windblown wingding," "run-on record" and "The Chicago Firestorm." The Philadelphia Inquirer chose a football analogy.

The Philadelphia Inquirer

sports

section C

◆◆◆ Friday, May 18, 1979

Phils win on extra point, 23-22

Schmidt's home run in the 10th inning makes the difference

By Jayson Stark
Inquirer Staff Writer

CHICAGO — The way the wind was blowing at Wrigley Field yesterday, you didn't need a Ph.D. in meteorology to know it was not going to be one of those 1-0, hour-and-33-minute pitchers' duels.

But you would have had to be Andy Warhol to figure that four hours later, the Cubs and Phillies would have put together a mere 44 runs, 49 hits, 29 singles, 10 doubles, two triples, 10 homers, 14 walks, four intentional walks, one hit batsman and five hit-arounds and used 11 pitchers.

And even after all that, nobody that should have been staged by the plate for the Phillies was Mike Schmidt. And Mike Schmidt specializes in games like this. On April 16, 1977, he hit four home runs in the same park on the same kind of day. Well, almost. That game was kind of low-scoring — only 18-16.

On this day, Schmidt worked the count to 3-and-2, found himself looking at a Bruce Sutter split-fingered pitch that wasn't split-fingering and orbited it over the bleachers in left-center.

And thus the Phillies won a game that should have been staged by the Not Ready For Line Drive Players, 23-22. The run total was four short of the major-league record set in 1922 by the Phils and Cubs.

"I figured the day I hit the four home runs, that was pretty much as wild a game as you'd ever see in baseball," said Schmidt, who also had a jet-stream-aided homer in the first and now has 14 this year, 10 this month.

"But this one," said Mike Schmidt, "he . . .

HOME RUN HITTER Randy Lerch, being congratulated by Coach Billy DeMars, gave the Phillies a seemingly safe 7-0 lead in the first inning. Forty-three hits, 38 runs and nearly four hours later, the Phillies finally had their victory.

No breeze

Eleven home runs were gone with the Wrigley wind

By Jayson Stark
Inquirer Staff Writer

CHICAGO — They don't have 23-22 games in the Astrodome . . . r . . . e . . . have 23 . . .

blowing 17 miles per hour at Wrigley Field and the direction it's h . . . is straight ov . . . th . . .

figured Del Unser, who played left field for the Phillies On the home . . .

hanging the ball around like that, on . . .her really looks good"

. . . swooping

Phillies-Cubs
May 17, 1979

Philadelphia	ab	r	h	rbi	Chicago	ab	r	h	rbi
McBride rf	8	2	3	1	DeJesus ss	6	4	3	1
Bowa ss	8	4	5	1	Vail rf	5	2	3	1
Rose 1b	7	4	3	4	Burris p	0	0	0	0
Schmidt 3b	4	3	2	4	Thompson cf	2	1	1	0
Unser lf	7	1	1	2	Buckner 1b	7	3	4	7
G.Maddox cf	4	3	4	4	Kingman lf	6	4	3	6
Gross cf	2	1	1	1	Ontiveros 3b	7	1	1	1
Boone c	4	2	3	5	Martin cf	6	2	3	3
Meoli 2b	5	0	1	0	Sutter p	0	0	0	0
Lerch p	1	1	1	1	Foote c	6	1	3	1
Bird p	1	1	0	0	Sizemore 2b	4	2	2	1
Luzinski ph	0	0	0	0	Caudill p	0	0	0	0
Espinosa pr	1	1	0	0	Murcer rf	2	0	1	0
McGraw p	0	0	0	0	Lamp p	0	0	0	0
Reed p	0	0	0	0	Moore p	1	0	1	1
McCarver ph	1	0	0	0	Hernandez p	1	0	0	0
Eastwick p	0	0	0	0	Dillard 2b	1	2	1	0
					Biittner ph	1	0	0	0
					Kelleher 2b	1	0	0	0
Total	53	23	24	23	Total	56	22	26	22

Philadelphia	708	240	100	1 - 23 - 24 - 2
Chicago	600	373	030	0 - 22 - 26 - 2

E-Schmidt 2, Kingman, DeJesus. DP-Philadelphia 2. LOB-Philadelphia 15, Chicago 7. 2B-Bowa 2, Maddox 2, Rose 2, Foote, Martin, DeJesus, Boone. 3B-Moore, Gross. HR-Kingman 3 (12), Schmidt 2 (14), Boone (2), Lerch (1), Maddox (6), Ontiveros (1), Buckner (4), Martin (3). SB-Bowa, Meoli. SF-Unser, Gross.

Philadelphia	IP	H	R	ER	BB	SO
Lerch	1-3	5	5	5	0	0
Bird	3 2-3	8	4	4	0	2
McGraw	2-3	4	7	4	3	1
Reed	3 1-3	9	6	6	0	0
Eastwick W, 1-0	2	0	0	0	0	1

Chicago	IP	H	R	ER	BB	SO
Lamp	1-3	6	6	6	0	0
Moore	2	6	7	7	2	1
Hernandez	2 2-3	7	8	6	7	1
Caudill	1 1-3	3	1	1	2	3
Burris	1 2-3	1	0	0	0	1
Sutter L, 1-1	2	1	1	1	1	0

HBP-by Hernandez (Boone). T-4:03. A-14,952.

---

giving dinner. Lerch served up a letter-high fastball on the outside corner that Kingman creamed. The blast began Kingman's personal assault on Waveland Avenue that day, as the ball hit the side of a building just a few feet below its roof. The Cubs closed the opening inning at 7–6 on three impressive line drive hits, the last a triple from Moore himself.

The Cubs lost a chance to take the lead in the bottom of the second because Kingman hit the ball too hard. Mike Vail and Bill Buckner had singled themselves to first and third with none out, but Kingman ripped a Doug Bird sinker right at Schmidt, and the ten-time Gold Glove winner looked Vail back and still had time to turn the double play, killing the rally.

Donnie Moore was to become an outstanding closer for the Angels in the mid-1980s, and in 1984 Willie Hernandez would win the Cy Young and Most Valuable Player awards for the world champion Tigers, but they both got rocked in Philadelphia's eight-run third inning. With the Cubs outfielders playing with their backs against the ivy, Garry Maddox and Boone started the assault with bloop doubles that on any other day would have been routine flies. With one out Moore walked Bird. Bake McBride followed with yet another rainbow single, and then the Phillies really got serious. Larry Bowa's line single scored one, Rose's line double scored two, and after Hernandez came on and walked Schmidt intentionally, Maddox crushed a hanging curve into the bleachers in left center to score three. Trailing 15–6 and representing a pitching staff that had been rattled for 13 hits, four of them homers, Hernandez did the only thing that made any sense—he threw at Boone, hitting him on the thigh. But this was no day to intimidate hitters. By the end of the top of the third inning, Cubs' pitchers had faced 27 batters—the minimum for a nine-inning game.

In the fifth inning, Philadelphia's Tug McGraw walked into a pitcher's dream—a 12-run lead and an easy chance for a win. He walked more batters than he retired and gave up hits to more batters than he walked. When he left the game, the Phillies' lead was down to five.

Inexplicably, Hernandez was allowed to bat for himself and struck out in the Cubs' scoreless third before returning to the slaughter. Bowa's third hit of the game was followed by Rose's second double, and when Cubs second baseman Ivan DeJesus finally saw a ball he could reach, he couldn't get it out of his glove, blowing a double play that would have ended the inning. Maddox poked a double to right center to make it 17–6 but wrenched his ankle sliding into second and left the game after going four for four with two doubles, one homer, three runs scored, and four RBI in just $4\frac{2}{3}$ innings.

Bird threw a pitch over Kingman's head with one out and one on in the Cub fourth, then threw the next pitch over the plate. Kingman stoically smashed another bomb onto Waveland Avenue, and Steve Ontiveros followed with a homer to right on a hanging curve to make it 17–9. Jerry Martin came within five feet of a third straight homer, but Greg Gross hauled in his fly at the 400-foot sign to end the inning.

Phillies pitcher Nino Espinosa performed an unusual feat—even for this game—in the top of the fifth. He was a pinch runner and a batter in the same inning, yet he never threw a pitch in the game. Espinosa ran for Greg Luzinski, who had walked pinch hitting for Bird. Philadelphia scored four times on a bloop double by Bowa, another DeJesus miscue, and two sacrifice flies. The Phillies batted around for the third time in five innings, averaging nine batters per inning. Espinosa ended the rally with a ground out.

Tug McGraw, who saved two games in the 1980 World Series to give the Phillies their first world championship, came on in the fifth. "It's funny," McGraw said. "When you're sitting out there in the pen and you see the way things are going, you don't exactly beg to come in the game. And yet, all the time you're saying to yourself: 'Well, I *know* I could stop all of this foolishness.'

Phillies catcher Bob Boone has caught more games than anyone else, but rarely was he this busy. Boone was on base five times, greeted 59 Cubs' hitters, and watched 22 of them cross the plate.

Losing in ten innings after overcoming a 12-run deficit was certainly a crime, but there were too many suspects, so Chicago's finest just had a ball like everyone else.

"So what happens? I get my chance to stop it, and blowie!" With two on and none out, McGraw walked Steve Dillard and DeJesus, who came into the game hitting a combined .191, then grooved a 2–1 fastball to Buckner, who lined it two-thirds of the way up the bleachers in right center for his second career grand slam. The eighth homer of the game, it cut the Phillies' lead to a touchdown, 21–14. Kingman stepped up, and McGraw looked as if he didn't want to let go of the ball. He did let go, but got it nowhere near the plate. With Kingman on first, Jerry Martin skied a low fastball into the second row in center field to chase McGraw and cut the lead to five.

Bowa's fifth hit and Schmidt's fourth walk were wasted in the Philly sixth, and the Cubs struck for three in their half of the inning. Just when Greg Gross decided he'd been playing too deep, DeJesus lined a double over his head after Dillard singled. Both scored on ground outs, and Kingman tapped a belt-high fastball from Ron Reed onto the porch of the fourth house along on Waveland, his longest shot of the day. Property values plunged, but the Cubs cut the lead to just two runs, 21–19. Boone's run-scoring double made the seventh inning the first single-run inning of the game and gave the Phillies a three-run lead.

In Schmidt's 1976 four-homer game, the Phillies—having trailed by 11 runs, 13–2—set a major league record for the biggest comeback win. In the bottom of the eighth the Cubs threatened to break the record again, tying the game with three runs off Reed. After pinch hitter Bobby Murcer stranded two runners with a ground out to second, Rose slammed the ball into the ground, then yapped at some fans on his way into the dugout. Catcher Barry Foote, who watched six Cubs' pitchers hand out 12 walks in the game, trudged back behind the plate to start the ninth. "I got so tired," Foote said, "I couldn't put my fingers down anymore."

Cubs shortstop Ivan DeJesus toured the bases four times but gave back a few runs with his sloppy fielding in the fourth and fifth, while Chicago's boys of summer (right) caught the action—and some rays.

The Cubs' Bruce Sutter brought his famed split-finger fastball to the mound in the top of the ninth. Sutter managed to end his half of the inning with Rudy Meoli stranded at third and the score tied. Rawley Eastwick, another split-finger specialist, set the Cubs down in order in their half and brought the game the only thing it lacked—a continuance. After 109 at-bats, and after the Phillies had blown leads of seven, eight, eleven and twelve runs, this most improbable of games defied probability once more and extended itself to extra innings. With two outs in the tenth, Schmidt stepped to the plate for the eighth time. Though light-hitting Del Unser was on deck, walking Schmidt would violate another cardinal rule—never put the winning run on base. And in most instances, Sutter's split-finger fastball made great hitters look ordinary. "Bruce Sutter walk me? Sutter ain't gonna walk anybody in this league with that pitch he's got," Schmidt said. But Sutter got the pitch up and in, and Schmidt hit it out. "I didn't even turn around to look at it," Sutter said. "I knew where it was going."

By the bottom of the tenth, Kingman had run out of heroics and fanned on a change-up. After four hours and three minutes of baseball, it was over. Despite the offensive onslaught, only one major league record was broken: most total bases by both clubs, 97. The top individual performances came from the losing Cubs, as Kingman scored four runs and drove in six, and Buckner had four hits and seven RBI. The 11 home runs tied a major league mark and gave Phillies general manager Paul Owens back his ulcer. "It took me two years to get rid of this damn ulcer, and it came back in three innings."

If the game proved anything, it is that while there may be a totally safe lead in a baseball game, no team has attained it yet. It was, as Philadelphia *Bulletin* reporter Mark Whicker wrote, "the day skepticism died." ◑

When a caveman wanted to kill his game, he didn't throw a rock at it, he beat it to death with a stick." Sound defensive? Consider the source: a pitcher, namely Bob Gibson, the great St. Louis Cardinals Hall of Famer. Gibson knows whereof he speaks. Every working day of his career, he faced strong men ready to beat him with their sticks.

Stick and ball games have been played for centuries on all continents. Images of people playing bat and ball games date back to ancient Egypt, pre-Columbian American cultures, medieval Europe, and the steppes of central Asia. In the American colonies, audacious children were chided for playing "stool ball," or "base," on the Sabbath. Those games evolved into club baseball by the 1830s—and although Abner Doubleday had nothing to do with it, organized baseball was an established pastime by the end of our Civil War.

The Stick and the Ball

Baseball has always served the hitter. In its earliest form, the "server" tossed the ball underhand, more or less where the "striker" called for it. Now Dwight Gooden challenges batters with pitches over 90 mph. But baseball games have always started with the pitcher delivering the ball to the plate, and not until the batter steps into the pitch does the drama begin.

"Hitting is the most important part of the game," says Ted Williams, who hit .406 in 1941. "It is where the big money is, where much of the status is, and the fan interest." And among hitters, the slugger commands unequaled attention. With one swing of the bat, José Canseco can drive a ball 400 feet, instantly turning a game around. But the slugger was not always synonymous with the home run hitter. In fact, through the 19th and early 20th centuries, the home run was an oddity, an aberration in a low-scoring, calculated game of well-placed hits, speed on the bases, and Herculean pitching efforts. The "dead-ball

Detroit's Kirk Gibson hit two home runs in Game 5 of the 1984 World Series, but San Diego pitcher Andy Hawkins was not one of his victims. The Tigers won the game 8–4 and the Series four games to one.

Tiger center fielder Ty Cobb was by far the liveliest and fiercest hitter of the dead-ball era.

In 1901, Cincinnati's Sam Crawford led the league with 16 homers, but his 16 triples ranked only fifth best.

era" it was called, and for good reason. Not until 1910 did a baseball have cork at its core. In that year the ball became "lively," and the old "hit and run" style of baseball was doomed. Although it took a few more years and a hero by the name of George Herman "Babe" Ruth to prove just how lively that ball could be, the old dead-ball game was not without its hard-hitting batters. Ty Cobb, who in a career that lasted from 1905 through 1928 hit only 118 home runs, was no less a slugger in his day for his lack of homers. Cobb's slugging was measured by his ability to drive in timely runs. In his 24 seasons he drove in 1,961 of them, putting him fourth on the all-time RBI list.

When Cobb broke into baseball, bats were heavy and baseballs soft. A single ball could be used for a whole game, sometimes several games in a row. When balls went into the stands, fans threw them back. Whatever life that dead ball had was beaten from it quickly. After a few innings—not to mention the end of a game—virtually all the power in a long, hard hit was supplied by the batter. Back then, it would not have been inaccurate to say that Cobb "slugged a single" to drive in the winning run.

Which is not to say that distance did not contribute to a slugger's stature or make for exciting moments in old-time baseball. "Wahoo" Sam Crawford, who played alongside the legendary Cobb in the Detroit outfield from 1905 through 1917, was the first man ever to lead both the National and American leagues in home runs, with sixteen and seven, respectively. But it was the triple that made Crawford famous. Crawford's 312 career three-baggers is still the all-time record; Cobb's 297 is second. In 1912, the Pirates' Owen Wilson hit 36 triples, still the major league season record. But not since Kiki Cuyler of the Pirates smashed 26 triples in 1925 has a player hit even as many as 24 in a single year.

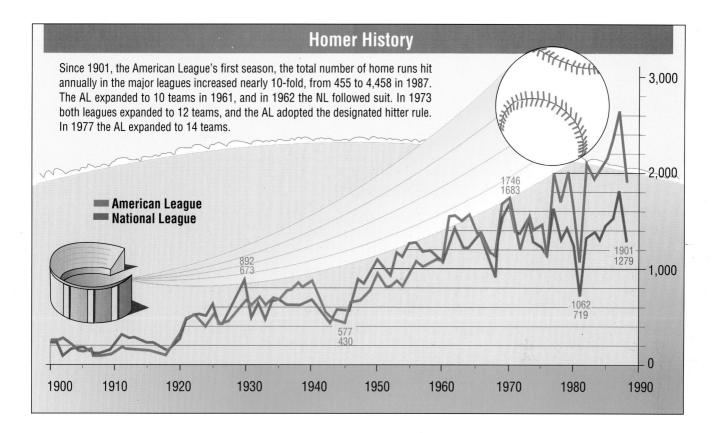

Homer History

Since 1901, the American League's first season, the total number of home runs hit annually in the major leagues increased nearly 10-fold, from 455 to 4,458 in 1987. The AL expanded to 10 teams in 1961, and in 1962 the NL followed suit. In 1973 both leagues expanded to 12 teams, and the AL adopted the designated hitter rule. In 1977 the AL expanded to 14 teams.

■ **American League**
■ **National League**

1746
1683

892
673

1901
1279

1062
719

577
430

3,000

2,000

1,000

0

1900 1910 1920 1930 1940 1950 1960 1970 1980 1990

Before the turn of the century, many parks were without fenced-in boundaries, and the outfielder's only defense against the long ball was to play back, way back. Whatever Ruth and the over-the-fence homer changed in the game of baseball, the one constant slugging feat over the years has been the clutch hit—the timely, do-or-die stroke. And there were times when that hit was a homer. Take the 1911 World Series, for example.

Game 1 was typical of the dead-ball days. The Giants of John McGraw took Connie Mack's Philadelphia Athletics 2–1, with the incomparable Christy Mathewson besting Chief Bender. In all there were 11 hits, mostly singles. In Game 2, Frank Baker, the American League's leading home run hitter that year—he hit 11—rocked a dramatic sixth-inning, two-out, two-run homer to break a 1–1 tie, giving the Athletics a 3–1 lead that held up through game's end. The next day Baker did it again, but in even more dramatic fashion, drilling a Mathewson, bottom-of-the-ninth fastball into the right field stands of the Polo Grounds and sending the game into extra innings. No matter that Philly eventually won it with two runs in the eleventh, and that in his 13-year career, Baker hit a total of 96 major league homers. For those two round trippers—and for a third he hit in the 1913 Series—the nickname "Home Run" has stuck to Frank Baker forever.

Baker's feats were nearly unheard of. Not only had he slugged decisive home runs in back-to-back Series games, but both homers had cleared the fences. For the fan in the stands back then, the slugging feat of choice was still an inside-the-park home run, pushing to the limit a player's ability and the fans' enthusiasm. It still brings a crowd to its feet. Today's inside-the-park four-baggers, rare as they are, call for distance hitting, speed, a daring recklessness, and superb timing.

Dead-ball era sluggers had to have speed, and Frank "Home Run" Baker was no exception. He had 96 career home runs but 235 steals.

New York Giant center fielder Casey Stengel beats the throw from Yankee shortstop Ernie Johnson to catcher Wally Schang on his Game 1-winning inside-the-park homer in the 1923 World Series. But in Game 3 Stengel strolled across the plate, as his seventh-inning homer carried into Yankee Stadium's right field bleachers and gave the Giants a 1–0 win.

No inside-the-park homer is more famous than the one Casey Stengel hit against the New York Yankees in Game 1 of the 1923 World Series. Stengel, who ten years earlier had hit the first home run in the history of Ebbets Field, also hit the first World Series homer in Yankee Stadium, which was less than a year old when the Series opened.

With two out and the score tied 4–4 in the top of the ninth inning, Stengel worked Yankee reliever Joe Bush to a 3-and-2 count. And then he connected, driving the next pitch into the furthest reaches of left center field, where Whitey Witt chased it down. Witt relayed the ball to Bob Meusel, whose arm was one of the strongest in the game. What happened next can be told only by one who was there. Here's how Damon Runyon, one of the great names in baseball literature, described the next few seconds in the New York *American* as the 34-year-old, bowlegged Stengel made his way around the bases.

> This is the way old Casey Stengel ran. . . .
> His mouth wide open.
> His warped old legs bending beneath him at every stride.
> His arms flying back and forth like those of a man swimming with a crawl stroke.
> His flanks heaving, his breath whistling, his head far back.
> Yankee infielders say Casey was muttering to himself, adjuring himself to greater speed, as a jockey mutters to his horse in a race, that he was saying, "Go on, Casey! Go on!"
> People—60,000 of 'em, men and women—were standing in the Yankee stands and bleachers up there in the Bronx roaring sympathetically, whether they were for or against the Giants.

Pittsburgh outfielder Kiki Cuyler is proof that sluggers weren't always home run hitters. In 1925, he hit just 17 homers, but his extra-base power gave him the second best slugging average in the league—.593.

"Come on, Casey!"

The warped old legs, twisted and bent by many a year of baseball campaigning, just barely held out under Casey Stengel until he reached the plate, running his home run home.

Then they collapsed. . . .

Half a dozen Giants rushed forward to help Casey to his feet, to hammer him on the back, to bawl congratulations in his ears as he limped unsteadily, still panting furiously, to the bench.

Stengel hit another game-winning homer in Game 3, but Ruth and the Yankees dominated the remainder of the Series. Although neither fans nor players realized it at the time, Stengel's homer served as a belated swan song to the dead-ball style of slugging. Babe Ruth had officially put the lid on those days in 1919 when he hit 29 home runs for the Boston Red Sox. Our notion of the slugger has never been the same.

The dead ball died for good in the 1920s.

Whatever its origins, baseball as we know it today is more elemental, more visceral—despite the computer-generated strategy and increased specialization position by position—than the games from which it evolved. Cricket, the English sport most Americans know in name only, perhaps has the most in common with baseball. A different kind of hitting and running game, cricket survived the American Revolution and was played regularly here until the new game lured American cricketers away in the 1840s and '50s. It takes an Englishman to finger the pulse of America's baseball and applaud, in baseball's favor, the wonderful difference between the two.

New York Mets right fielder Darryl
Strawberry (above) and British cricket star
Ian Botham (above right) show it's not what
bat you swing, but how hard you swing it,
that counts.

Since it was built in 1923, Yankee Stadium
(opposite) has always been both an inviting
and imposing home run park. At 318 feet to
left and 314 feet to right, it's a pull-hitter's
delight, but its power alleys—399 in left
center and 385 in right center—are among
the game's roomiest.

"Baseball reflects American society's need for confrontation," writes W.J.
Weatherby in the English newspaper the *Manchester Guardian.* "If you go to
Yankee Stadium or Shea Stadium you must forget all about cricket. The
noisiest crowd quiets down when Strawberry steps up to face a pitcher. The
suspense is electric as everyone waits to see if this is one of those days when
the loose-limbed young giant will hit another homer out of the ground. If
player after player is struck out without scoring, the yearning for a homer
creates an almost unbearable tension."

The source of that yearning, of course, is the world's greatest sports
hero: Babe Ruth. Ruth was to baseball what Einstein was to physics; he rode
the home run to international fame and legend, even in countries where
baseball was barely pronounceable, let alone comprehensible. For three consecutive seasons the Babe performed the unthinkable, as he hit 29, 54 and 59
homers in 1919, '20 and '21, respectively. And in 1927 he slugged a magical 60
homers. Some baseball purists bemoaned the loss of the hit-and-scratch
game, the playing for one run at a time. They complained that hitting home
runs in such numbers was crude and excessive, underscoring the lapse in skill
that would be epidemic in baseball unless the deft bat-handling of a former
time was reinstituted. They overlooked the fact that Ruth was more than a
home run hitter. In addition to 714 career home runs, he had a .342 *lifetime*
batting average. Ruth was every bit as large as the legend, and he was capable
of carrying the burden of change of the hitting game to the slugging one.

No player ever felt the weight of that burden more than Roger Maris did
in 1961. Thirty-four years after Ruth's record 60 homers, Maris made an un-
forgettable run of his own toward the greatest slugging record of the century.
In the course of his 61-homer season, Maris was criticized by fans as well as

The M&M Boys—New York Yankees Maris and Mantle

Great One-Two Punches

They are every manager's dream, every pitcher's nightmare. Wedged together in the middle of the lineup, they form a hill pitchers must climb four or five times each game, and each time it's a little steeper.

From Ruth and Gehrig of the Yankees to Canseco and McGwire of the Athletics, just about every consistently successful team has had them—power hitters whose back-to-back placement makes the whole lineup more productive and harder to pitch to. They are baseball's version of boxing's one-two punch. Those who bat before them see lots of nice fat strikes; those who bat behind them face pitchers who are either shell-shocked or dangerously complacent. In the primary confrontation between pitcher and batter, the pitcher holds both a physical and a psychological edge. This edge can, however, be blunted from the on-deck circle. Pitching to Hank Aaron was tough. Pitching to Aaron with Eddie Mathews in the corner of your eye was downright unnerving.

Aaron and Mathews are baseball's all-time best one-two punch—combining for 863 home runs and 2,633 RBI in 13 seasons with Milwaukee and Atlanta. In many ways they were the perfect tandem. Aaron hit right handed, Mathews left handed. Mathews' power made it foolish to pitch around Aaron, and Aaron's speed distracted pitchers and opened holes in the infield for Mathews.

Having power hitters back to back helps both pile up bigger numbers. Among the top 20 all-time home run hitters are five one-two punches—Ruth and Gehrig, Boston's Jimmie Foxx and Ted Williams, Aaron and Mathews, Mays and McCovey, and Chicago's Ernie Banks and Billy Williams.

But greater than the effect they have on each other is the effect tandem power hitters have on the opposition. They force the action from the first pitch. Managers stack the one-two slots in their lineup with "table-setters"—high-average hitters with speed, patience, and good bat control. Pitchers must keep these guys off base but must walk a fine

The Bay Area has had its share of one-two punches. Oakland's Mark McGwire (near right) and Jose Canseco are baseball's newest home run duo, combining for 80 homers in 1987, while San Francisco's Willie Mays (24, below) and Willie McCovey combined for 91 homers in 1965.

line to do so. Pitch them tough and they'll get their share of walks; come right after them and they'll single you to death. With the right personnel, a manager can tip the balance of power toward his hitters before the game even starts.

Take the 1985 Yankees, for example. You're on the mound, and leading off is Rickey Henderson, who got on base 41 percent of the time. He also stole 80 bases, so when Willie Randolph steps to the plate there's a big hole on the right side of the infield and the pitcher's got one eye on Henderson. Randolph, a great bat handler, hit .276 and walked 85 times, so he's on base 39 percent of the time.

Now the trouble really starts. You've been harassed by Henderson and Randolph, and your confidence isn't what it ought to be. Bad news, because Don Mattingly's at the plate, and all 6'6" and 220 pounds of Dave Winfield is in the on-deck circle. Mattingly swings left handed, hits with power to all fields, and hardly ever strikes out. In 1985 he hit .324 with 35 homers and led the league with 145 RBI. After facing Mattingly's classic stroke from the left side, you now face Winfield's slashing, violent swing from the right side. Winfield hit .275 with 26 homers and 114 RBI that year, as the Yankees scored 5.21 runs per game, tops in the majors.

More often than not, these pairings lead to pennants. The 1957–58 Braves had Aaron and Mathews, while the Yankee dynasty had Gehrig and Ruth, DiMaggio and Tommy Henrich, and Mantle and Maris. In all, New York won 33 pennants in 67 years, inventing and then perfecting the concept of Murderers' Row.

Triple Crown Winners

The Triple Crown Award, given when a player leads his league in home runs, batting average and runs batted in during one season, is baseball's single greatest slugging achievement. Since 1878, only 14 players have won the Triple Crown.

National League

Year	Player	HR	BA	RBI
1878	Paul Hines, Providence	4	.358	50
1894	Hugh Duffy, Boston	18	.438	145
1912	Heinie Zimmerman, Chicago	14	.372	103
1922	Rogers Hornsby, St Louis	42	.401	152
1925	Rogers Hornsby, St Louis	39	.403	143
1933	Chuck Klein, Philadelphia	28	.368	120
1937	Joe Medwick, St Louis	31	.374	154

American League

Year	Player	HR	BA	RBI
1901	Napoleon Lajoie, Philadelphia	14	.422	125
1909	Ty Cobb, Detroit	9	.377	107
1933	Jimmie Foxx, Philadelphia	48	.356	163
1934	Lou Gehrig, New York	49	.363	165
1942	Ted Williams, Boston	36	.356	137
1947	Ted Williams, Boston	32	.343	114
1956	Mickey Mantle, New York	52	.353	130
1966	Frank Robinson, Baltimore	49	.316	122
1967	Carl Yastrzemski, Boston	44	.326	121

Equally dazzling at the plate and on the basepaths, Giant center fielder Willie Mays led the National League four times each in homers and steals.

by the press for being an unworthy challenger to the Babe. But Maris' intention had nothing to do with unseating Ruth or anyone else. He simply hit a groove that season and rode it out over the course of 162 games. No one since has even come close to matching Maris' 1961 performance.

The Maris assault on Ruth's single-season record simply called attention to what Maris could not sustain. No one really expected Maris to be another Babe Ruth, but it was clear that by 1961, a slugger must do more than merely hit homers. He must hit them heroically, as Ruth had, with power. And like Ruth, he must hit for average as well. Over the decades, a small but memorable fraternity of slugging greats proved that it could be done.

With the exception of Ruth, no one made the transition from dead-ball batter to lively-ball slugger better than Rogers Hornsby, who played 23 seasons for the Cardinals, Giants, Braves, Cubs, and Browns. Hornsby led the National League in hitting for six consecutive seasons, three times hitting over .400. From 1920 to 1925 Hornsby *averaged* .397; his .424 average in 1924 is the highest average of any player in the 20th century, and his .358 lifetime average is second only to Ty Cobb's .367. Hornsby hit 301 career homers—the first National Leaguer to hit as many as 300 in a career—including 42 and 39 in 1922 and 1925, respectively, when he won the National League Triple Crown, the only man to do so twice.

Hornsby's career overlapped those of other sluggers equal to the new calling: Jimmie Foxx, who in his last years teamed with young Ted Williams in Boston, hit .325 and 534 home runs in 20 seasons, including 58 in 1932; and Ruth's teammate Lou Gehrig, who played in a record 2,130 consecutive games, was a .340 lifetime hitter with 493 home runs. But it wasn't until 1951, 14 years after Hornsby's retirement, that a slugger came along who was

Second baseman Rogers Hornsby was the National League's slugging equivalent to Babe Ruth. In 1922, Hornsby hit .401 with 42 homers—a 40/.400 feat neither Ruth nor anyone else matched.

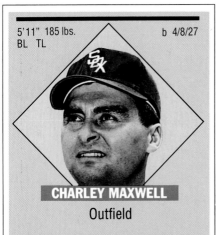

5'11" 185 lbs.
BL TL
b 4/8/27

CHARLEY MAXWELL
Outfield

Charley "Paw Paw" Maxwell was a journeyman outfielder who played 14 years in the majors with the Red Sox, Orioles, Tigers, and White Sox. Maxwell never led the league in any hitting category, and he never played on a pennant winner. And although he batted .326 with 28 homers for the Tigers in 1956, Maxwell is best remembered for his 1959 season when he hit 12 of his career high 31 home runs during Sunday ball games.

It started on May 3, 1959, a Sunday, of course. In the first game of a doubleheader against the Yankees, Maxwell went two for four, including a home run in his final at-bat, as Detroit defeated New York, 4–2. In the nightcap, Maxwell blasted homers in three consecutive official at-bats—he walked in his second plate appearance—to tie a record shared by Bobby Lowe, Lou Gehrig, Jimmie Foxx, Hank Greenberg, Bill Nicholson, Ralph Kiner, and Ted Williams.

Through the rest of May and June, Maxwell homered on the following Sundays: May 10, May 31, June 7, June 14 and June 28. What's more, every homer during that stretch either tied the game or won it for the Tigers.

By the All-Star break in July, Maxwell was something of a legend in the American League, earning the nickname "The Sabbath Smasher." He concluded the '59 season with a .297 average in 28 Sunday games in which he drove in an incredible 33 runs. And to this day he swears he never went to church during the season.

capable of adding a dynamic new dimension to the role of slugger created by Ruth. His name was Willie Mays.

Mays was unique, and his style of play made him a hero of nearly Ruthian proportions. Others who followed him might surpass him in numbers or sheer ability—Henry Aaron hit 755 home runs to Mays' 660, and no player in history could match Mickey Mantle for sheer power and speed. Playing for the New York Giants in the wide open spaces of the old Polo Grounds, Mays had a certain flair that was apparent in every aspect of his game, from his inimitable "basket" catches, to throwing on the run, to losing his cap as he rounded a base to stretch a single into a double or triple. Mays made the running and fielding aspect of his game as important as it had been prior to Ruth, yet he managed to put the slugger's style into it as well. He ran as he hit—aggressively. And he was all slugger. Six times he hit 40 or more home runs in a season, and he is one of two National Leaguers—the other being Ralph Kiner—to hit 50 or more home runs in two separate seasons. He led the National League in stolen bases four consecutive years, and in 1955 he became the first player ever to hit at least 50 home runs and steal 20 bases in a single season. In 22 years in the majors he hit .302 and collected 3,283 hits.

By the time Mays was becoming a slugging legend, the home run had evolved into a prodigious offensive weapon, and the slugger was expected to deliver at will. Earl Weaver, who managed the Baltimore Orioles for 17 years, from the late 1960s through the 1980s, was famous for advocating the three-run homer as a strategic weapon instead of giving up an out to move a runner to scoring position. To deliver in the clutch the blast that will put his team ahead or win the game has always been the duty of the

The Detroit Tigers' Al Kaline (right) was one of the great right fielders of all time, but in 1974—his final season—he became a designated hitter and reached the hallowed 3,000-hit mark.

Don Baylor brought speed to the slow-footed profile of a designated hitter. He stole 20 or more bases eight times and had a career-high 52 steals in 1975 with Baltimore.

slugger. Increasingly through the late 1960s and 1970s, it became his one area of specialization.

Quite possibly no one player ever performed such a feat so well as one who never played in the majors, not because he didn't have the ability but because he was black. His name was Mule Suttles. In the days of the Negro leagues, when all black players—many of exceptional ability—were prohibited because of their color from playing in the major leagues, Suttles was one of baseball's all-time great sluggers. He was known for his long-distance homers and for delivering in the clutch and in tough situations, notably championship series and Negro League All-Star games, in which he compiled a .412 average and an incredible .883 slugging percentage. In his career, Suttles hit more homers than the now legendary Josh Gibson. He reportedly once hit three homers in a single inning of an East-West Negro League game.

But Suttles' fielding left a lot to be desired, an accusation—frequently unfounded—that sluggers both black and white, from Suttles to Ted Williams, have suffered for generations. Then the idea occurred to someone that a stone-fingered slugger was an unnecessary liability. Thus, in 1973, the designated hitter was born. And it was one of the biggest changes in the game since the introduction of the lively ball.

By the late 1960s, batting had reached a low point. In 1968 Carl Yastrzemski hit .301, making him the only .300 hitter in the American League, the lowest league-leading average in history. To Commissioner Bowie Kuhn and American League owners, the designated hitter made sense twice over: more offensive power—as well as more spectator interest.

In at least one sense, the DH rule—which allows for a nonfielding player

to hit in the pitcher's spot in the lineup—was a public relations attempt to restore interest in baseball. By the end of the 1960s the country's attention had been diverted from the baseball diamond to the war in Vietnam. Ignoring the fact that attendance at baseball games has been down during every war in this nation's history, the American League, opting for what seemed like a surefire elixir, voted in favor of the new rule in December of 1972. It was less than half a solution.

Slick-fielding center fielders Dale Murphy (above left) of the Atlanta Braves and Kirby Puckett of the Minnesota Twins are definitely not the designated hitter type. A two-time Most Valuable Player and the National League home run champ in 1984, Murphy has won five Gold Glove awards for his defense. Puckett, who hit .356 with 121 RBI in 1988, threw out more base runners—16—than any American League outfielder in 1984, his rookie season.

⬤n April 7, 1973, Ron Blomberg of the Yankees became the first designated hitter in history, drawing a bases-loaded walk off Boston's Luis Tiant in the bottom of the first. Blomberg was the prototypical DH. He was a strapping left-handed hitter who couldn't hit southpaws and couldn't play first base, the last repose of fielders who can no longer field. His nickname: "Dr. Clank."

Former Pirate outfielder and manger Bill Virdon expressed the sentiment of many who initially favored adding a tenth player to the lineup when he said, "It keeps your best hitters around longer." And at first it did, as such sluggers as Rico Carty, Harmon Killebrew, Tony Oliva, Al Kaline, and Hank Aaron closed out their careers in the DH role. But soon the DH became a specialist, as players with virtually no experience in the field became the designated hitters of the 1980s. Although such players as Hal McRae, Greg Luzinski, and Don Baylor were legitimate sluggers, each seemed like only half the player he should be.

But oddly enough, everything that is unpopular about the DH rule may have inspired the best of today's sluggers to rise above any fielding limitations and attempt to master, if not excel in, their defensive roles. Back in the 1970s,

The Tigers' Gates Brown

The Pinch Hitter

f, as Ted Williams says, hitting a baseball is the single hardest feat in sports, then how hard is pinch hitting? Too hard.

The pinch hitter's lot is much like that of a field goal kicker. After sitting on the bench for most of the game, he's asked to produce in what is probably the game's most pressure-packed moment.

He is probably facing the other team's bullpen stopper, who more often than not has a 90-mile-per-hour fastball, and he probably hasn't swung a bat for three hours. Unlike anyone else in the lineup, he's got only one at-bat to succeed. Few pinch hitters succeed consistently, so those who do have become a sort of fraternity in the clutch.

The term *pinch hitter* originated in the 1910s, when dependable hitters were expected to perform minor miracles "in a pinch." Who was the best pinch hitter ever? Probably Manny Mota, who tops the all-time list with 150 career pinch hits. Mota hit .297 as a pinch hitter for the Giants, Pirates, Expos, and Dodgers. The last seven years of his career were spent almost exclusively as a pinch hitter, and during that period he hit .315. Mota personified the concentration and calm all good pinch hitters need. "He could wake up on Christmas morning and rip a single into right field," wrote Jim Murray of the *Los Angeles Times*.

But Mota was the exception. For most, coming cold off the bench into a pressure situation was the stuff .200 hitters are made of. The aging Ty Cobb hit .217 in 69 at-bats as a pinch hitter, and Babe Ruth hit .194 in 67 tries. Pinch hitting often got the best of great hitters because the deck is stacked against them. Smokey Burgess, a rotund catcher who produced 16 homers among his 145 career pinch hits, said, "You haven't been in the game, you haven't had a chance to limber up, you haven't had a chance to see what stuff the pitcher has, and it's usually a clutch situation."

Rusty Staub was another exception. A high-average hitter throughout his career, Staub knocked in 28 runs on 24 pinch hits in 1983 for the New York Mets, tying Jerry Lynch and Joe Cronin for most RBI by a pinch hitter. Staub's preparation was key to his success. "Rusty Staub was more prepared to get up and get a base hit than anyone I've ever seen," said Cubs manager Jim Frey. "Rusty caught the subtle things. He could tell a pitch by the way a fellow took the ball out of his glove—one way fastball, another way breaking ball—or by the way he stuck the ball into the glove."

If Mota wasn't the best pinch hitter ever, then Lynch was. His late-inning bat was a powerful weapon for Cincinnati in the late '50s and early '60s. Lynch led the National League in pinch hit appearances with 66 in 1960 and holds the NL mark for career pinch hit homers with 18.

Some pinch hitters, like Dusty Rhodes, have

New York Giants teammates mobbed Dusty Rhodes after his pinch-hit homer won Game 1 of the 1954 World Series.

had remarkable single seasons highlighted by postseason heroics. Rhodes pinch hit .333 for the New York Giants in 1954 and led the Giants to a World Series sweep with three pinch hits and six RBI, including a pinch three-run homer to win the Series opener. But then Rhodes, a lifetime .211 pinch hitter, reverted to form and hit just .250 as a pinch hitter in 1955. Detroit's Gates Brown also experienced one phenomenal year as a pinch hitter. In 1968 Brown pinch hit .462 for the world champion Tigers but surrounded that season with a .154 mark in 1967 and .205 in 1969.

The major leagues' top pinch hitter of all time, Manny Mota was as versatile as he was durable. In a 20-year career, Mota hit .304—seven points higher than his pinch hitting average—and played the outfield, third base, second base, and catcher.

Mike Greenwell is the latest in a long line of sluggers—Ted Williams, Carl Yastrzemski, Jim Rice—to play left field in Boston's Fenway Park.

sluggers like Kent Hrbek of the Minnesota Twins or Pete Incaviglia of the Texas Rangers would have found their names automatically penciled in the DH position of the lineup. No longer.

Today's slugger, in both the National and American leagues, recognizes that the fan, too, is inspired only by the complete player. Kirby Puckett, Dale Murphy, Andre Dawson, Don Mattingly, Dave Winfield, Jose Canseco—each represents the new slugger of the 1980s, the complete baseball player.

"You used to have guys stressing different jobs," says Lee May, who hit 354 homers from 1965 to 1982. "You had big guys who struck out and hit home runs. Now everybody wants to do everything. In the era of technology, everybody is trying to be that supreme hitter." The Babe would be proud. ⦿

At 6'6", 220 lbs., Yankee rightfielder Dave Winfield is one of just a few players who can physically dominate a baseball game. A superb athlete, Winfield swings, runs and throws as hard as anyone.

Ted Williams

"All I want out of life is to be able to walk down the street and have people point at me and say, 'There goes the greatest hitter who ever lived.'"

Five players had better career batting averages than Ted Williams, and seven hit more home runs. Twelve had more total bases, and nine of those twelve drove in more runs. He holds few lifetime and single-season major league batting records, and in what was probably his best season he wasn't even named Most Valuable Player. Yet many informed observers agree that Williams got his wish.

Williams was spectacular in his consistency—only Babe Ruth matched Williams' prowess in all phases of hitting. In seasons in which he had at least 400 at-bats, Williams never hit below .318. He hit 30 or more homers eight times, scored and drove in 100 or more runs nine times, and had 100 or more walks eleven times. He won two Triple Crowns, two Most Valuable Player awards, and had a lifetime on-base percentage of .480.

In 1941 at the age of 23, Williams became the first player to hit over .400 since Bill Terry in 1930 and is the last to break the .400 plateau. At age 39 Williams came within five hits of .400 again as he won his fifth batting title with a .388 average and hit 38 homers—100 points and 16 homers more than Ruth hit at that age. Then, just to show it was no

fluke, he won his sixth batting crown the following season.

If he is the best hitter ever, Williams would say it was because he worked harder than anyone else. "Choose any of the noted hitters," he wrote in his autobiography *My Turn at Bat,* "and none of them hit any more balls, swung a bat in practice more times than Theodore Samuel Williams."

Growing up in southern California allowed Williams ample opportunity to practice his passion: hitting baseballs. A .430 hitter in high school, Williams signed with the San Diego Padres of the Pacific Coast League in 1936 and with the Red Sox in 1937. Tall, skinny and cocky, Williams burned up the minors in 1938 with a .366 average, 43 homers, and 142 RBI. He led the American League with 145 RBI his rookie year and hit .327 with 31 homers and 107 walks.

In 1941, Williams' pursuit of .400 didn't take center stage until after Joe DiMaggio's 56-game hitting streak ended in mid-July, but it held every bit as much drama. Williams went into the Red Sox' season-ending three game series in Philadelphia batting .401 but in a 2-for-11 slump. Red Sox manager Joe Cronin offered to let Williams sit out

Williams' picture-perfect swing included total follow-through.

the series in order to preserve his .400 average, but Williams declined. "Either I make it or I don't."

"You got to admire the kid for being so courageous about it," Cronin said. "But I can tell you one thing, I may yank him in that second game Sunday if he's got his hits. It'll be pretty dark when that second game gets under way and I may decide to take him out even if he doesn't like it."

Athletics manager Connie Mack started Roger Wolff, a rookie knuckleballer who had pitched a three-hitter in his first major league start, in Saturday's game. In that game Williams went one for four against Wolff, extending his slump to three for his last fifteen.

When he stepped to the plate in the second inning of the first game in Sunday's doubleheader, Philadelphia catcher Frankie Hayes said to him, "I wish you all the luck in the world, Ted. But Mr. Mack told us he'd run us out of baseball if we let up on you. You're going to have to earn it." Williams nodded, then began one of the most famous one-day performances in baseball history.

He singled to right in the second and hit a 440-foot homer—his 37th of the season—in the fifth, both off Dick Fowler. Porter Vaughn fared no bet-

ter, as Williams singled twice to right off the Athletics' left hander before reaching on an error in the ninth. The Red Sox won 12–11, and Williams' four for five performance in the first game boosted his average to .404. The milestone was secure—only going zero for six in the second game could drop Williams below .400. But Williams went two for three in the nightcap—which was called after eight innings because of darkness—including a double off the loudspeaker atop Shibe Park's right center field wall. He ended the season at .406 with 37 homers and 120 RBI.

The following year Williams won his first Triple Crown; he spent the next three years in the Navy. When Williams returned in 1946, Cleveland manager Lou Boudreau greeted him with a new defense. It was devised to keep the left-handed Williams from pulling the ball to right. Boudreau shifted his shortstop to the right side of the infield, leaving the third baseman alone midway between second and third and daring Williams to hit to the opposite field. Other teams followed suit. Despite the shift, Williams hit .342 with 38 homers and 123 RBI. But in one of his greatest personal disappointments, Williams hit just .200 in his only World Series

*Williams (right) got congratulations
from Joe DiMaggio (5) and coach
Marv Shea (30) for his game-winning
homer in the 1941 All-Star Game,
and (above) from his son, John Henry,
for managing the Senators in 1969 to
their first .500 season since 1953.*

as the Red Sox lost to the Cardinals in seven games.

Williams had an often stormy relationship with the press, who criticized him for not hitting to left field against the shift, for his cockiness, and for what they perceived as his inability to hit in big games. In addition to his poor World Series performance, Williams got just one hit in Boston's 8–3 loss to Cleveland in a 1948 playoff game for the pennant, and in 1949 he went hitless in the final two games of the season as the Red Sox lost a one-game lead and the pennant to the Yankees. But Red Sox fans loved him, even when his temper got the best of him, as it did in 1956 when his habit of spitting at fans induced owner Thomas Yawkey to threaten Williams with a $5,000 fine.

Williams shone in All-Star games, hitting .304 in 18 games, and is the all-time leader in RBI and walks. In 1941 he hit a three-run homer with two out in the bottom of the ninth to give the American League a 7–5 win, and in 1946 he led a 12–0 AL romp with two homers, the last coming off an eephus—or blooper—pitch by Pittsburgh's Rip Sewell. It was the first homer hit off Sewell's eephus—a pitch that rose 25 feet in the air on its way from the mound.

In 1960 Williams capped a brilliant career with a home run in his last at-bat and took off for Florida to enjoy his second love—fishing. He was inducted into the Hall of Fame in 1966 and returned to baseball in 1969 as manager of the Washington Senators. He led the Senators to their first .500 finish since they entered the American League as an expansion team in 1961. The team's batting average rose 27 points and its run total 170. Williams was named Manager of the Year.

While Stan Musial can probably lay claim as hitting's evolutionary link between Ty Cobb and Don Mattingly, Williams was one of the first to approach hitting as a science, and he elevated it to an art. His swing, with its powerful hip rotation, was as close to Ruth's as any, but Williams was two inches taller and twenty-five pounds lighter than the Babe and had a longer stroke. He had more power than Cobb or Musial and struck out much less frequently than Ruth.

A tireless student of the game, Williams had an uncanny knack for reading pitchers' minds. "I didn't have to keep a written book on pitchers. I lived a book on pitchers," he said.

Williams studied the whole field but almost always hit to right, even after teams employed drastic shifts to stop him.

TED
WILLIAMS

Outfield
Boston Red Sox 1939–1942,
    1946–1960
Hall of Fame 1966

GAMES	2,292
AT-BATS	7,706
BATTING AVERAGE	
Career *(7th all time)*	.344
Season High	.406
BATTING TITLES	**1941, 1942**
	1947, 1948, 1957, 1958
SLUGGING AVERAGE	
Career *(2nd all time)*	.634
Season High *(10th all time)*	.735
HITS	
Career	2,654
Season High	194
DOUBLES	
Career	525
Season High	44
TRIPLES	
Career	71
Season High	14
HOME RUNS	
Career *(10th all time)*	521
Season High	43
TOTAL BASES	4,884
EXTRA BASE HITS	1,117
RUNS BATTED IN	
Career *(10th all time)*	1,839
Season High	159
RUNS	
Career	1,798
Season High	150
WORLD SERIES	1946
MOST VALUABLE PLAYER	
	1946, 1949

The Babe

Babe Ruth hit three home runs in Game 4 in 1926 to set a World Series record against the St. Louis Cardinals, including this first-inning blast off Flint Rhem. Two years later he tied his own record, also in Game 4 against the Cardinals.

Babe Ruth

Ruth's home run trot—like everything else about him—was inimitable. His mincing, almost delicate steps as he circled the bases belied his awesome power.

The 1927 American League pennant race was a runaway, with the New York Yankees winning a record 110 games and finishing a full 19 games ahead of Connie Mack's second place Philadelphia Athletics. But the delirium that gripped the city of New York when Mack brought his team to town on September 27 was no less heated than pennant fever. The Yankees' Babe Ruth was closing in on a new record of his own: 60 home runs in a single season. With four games left, the Babe needed a homer a game to do it, and no one was betting he wouldn't.

To be sure, Ruth wanted the record. Since being switched from pitcher to full-time outfielder with the Red Sox in 1918, Ruth seemed destined to break home run records. In 1919, he hit a record 29 homers. The following season, his first with the Yankees, he hit a phenomenal 54, and he eclipsed that in 1921 when he hit 59. For the next six seasons, no one even came close to matching Ruth's home run supremacy. But midway through the 1927 season, the first baseman who batted behind Ruth in the Yankee lineup, Lou Gehrig, was making a legitimate record run of his own. And when Gehrig hit his 38th of the season, a ninth-inning blast that stole a shutout from Philadelphia's Rube Walberg on August 10, John Nolan of the Philadelphia *Evening Bulletin* crowned Gehrig "the new home run king."

That homer put Columbia Lou three up on the Bambino, but it was also his last for the next ten days. By the end of the month the Babe had regained the lead, 42–41. Then on September 6, Ruth raised his total to 47 as he hit three homers in a doubleheader against the Red Sox. His first of the day was a mammoth blast that carried over the left center field wall of Fenway Park. Later, Ruth remembered that day as "the first time I believed I had a chance to make it. We had the pennant pretty well cinched and I could afford to do a

In the 1920s and 1930s, Philadelphia's Jimmie Foxx (center) and the Yankees' Lou Gehrig (left) and Ruth lambasted American League pitching. In addition to Ruth's single-season home run record in 1927, Gehrig set the AL record with 184 RBI in 1931 and Foxx set the record for most home runs by a right-handed hitter—58—in 1932.

In 1926, the St. Louis Cardinals met the Yankees in the World Series, bringing together baseball's two greatest hitters—Rogers Hornsby (left) and Ruth. Although Ruth outhomered Hornsby 4–0, St. Louis won the Series in seven games.

little hitting for myself. It was then that I got busy." The next day Ruth hit two more out of Fenway, and by September 22 his total stood at 56. Gehrig, in that same span, had hit but one.

The only headline Ruth managed during the next four days was the announcement of his intention to appear in a new film starring comedian Harold Lloyd. On the field, he was uncharacteristically restrained: a couple of singles and a rifle-throw from Yankee Stadium's right field corner to nail Detroit's Johnny Bassler trying to stretch a single into a double.

A modest Tuesday afternoon crowd of 15,000 turned out at Yankee Stadium to root the Babe to a record-breaking finish. But Yankee manager Miller Huggins had nothing but winning on his mind. Following Sunday's 6–1 humiliation at the hands of the fourth place Tigers and fearful the apathy his team showed against Detroit would carry over to the upcoming World Series, Huggins sent 17-game winner Herb Pennock to the mound against Philadelphia's Rube Walberg. The Athletics held a 4–2 lead after four innings, when Mack called 20-game winner Lefty Grove out of the bullpen. After touching Grove for a run in the fifth, the Yankees loaded the bases in the bottom of the sixth on a one-out single by Joe Dugan and two walks. But Grove tightened his grip on things and struck out Yankee shortstop Mark Koenig. Which brought up Ruth, who had gone homerless against Grove all season. The Babe hammered Grove's first pitch deep into the right field bleachers. It was Ruth's first grand slam of the season, and only his fourth as a Yankee. More importantly, it was his 57th home run of the year.

The Yankees were scheduled to end their season with a three-game series against the Washington Senators at home in Yankee Stadium. With the great Tris Speaker in center, Goose Goslin in left, and Sam Rice in right, it was

BABE RUTH

Outfield
Boston Red Sox 1914-1919
New York Yankees 1920-1934
Boston Braves 1935
Hall of Fame 1936

GAMES	2,503
AT BATS	8,399
BATTING AVERAGE	
Career	.342
Season High	.393
BATTING TITLES	1924
SLUGGING AVERAGE	
Career *(1st all time)*	.690
Season *(1st all time)*	.847
HITS	
Career	2,873
Season High	205
DOUBLES	
Career	506
Season High	45
TRIPLES	
Career	136
Season High	16
HOME RUNS	
Career *(2nd all time)*	714
Season High *(2nd all time)*	60
TOTAL BASES *(5th all time)*	5,793
EXTRA BASE HITS	
(3rd all time)	1,356
RUNS BATTED IN	
Career *(2nd all time)*	2,211
Season High *(7th all time)*	171
RUNS	
Career *(2nd all time)*	2,174
Season High *(2nd all time)*	177
WORLD SERIES	1915, 1916
1918, 1921-23, 1926-28, 1932	
MOST VALUABLE PLAYER	1923

On August 14, 1934, 74,000 fans at Yankee Stadium watched as Ruth slid in ahead of Detroit catcher Ray Hayworth's tag, but by then the Tigers had slid past the Yankees into first place. Underrated as a baserunner, Ruth had 123 career stolen bases, including 17 in both 1921 and 1923.

Washington's finest versus the Babe. Determined to see his third place Senators put an end to Ruth's run for the record, player-manager Bucky Harris started 18-game winner Horace Lisenbee in Thursday afternoon's opener. But the Senators failed to gain even a toehold to their standoff, as Ruth clubbed a first inning two-strike curve ball three rows into the right field bleachers, his 58th homer of the season. The Babe rocked another Lisenbee mistake for a triple—a near-miss homer off the right center field wall—in the Yankees' seven-run second. New York was up 11–4 and Lisenbee was gone and showered when Ruth came to bat in the fifth with the bases loaded. This time his victim was rookie right hander Paul Hopkins, who had all of five innings of major league pitching under his belt. Hopkins' rude induction into Ruth's legion of the abused was immediate, as the Babe took the rookie deep. It was his second grand slam in consecutive games and the ball landed in the same spot as the one he hit off Grove, a good 400 feet into the right field bleachers, tying his own existing record of 59 home runs. By day's end, Ruth had gone three for five with two homers, a triple, and seven RBI. And only a back-to-the-wall catch by Red Barnes, who had replaced Rice in right field, kept it from being a three-homer, record-breaking performance.

On Friday, September 30, Ruth ended the drama and the season, but not until he turned the 153rd game of the year into a major subplot all its own. Tom Zachary went the distance for Washington, going head to head with the Babe four times. Cast in the role of villain, the veteran Zachary lived up to the billing when he opened the game by walking Ruth on four straight pitches in the first, and 10,000 paying customers bellowed a resounding chorus of the Bronx Cheer. Ruth came to bat again in the fourth and sixth innings, and each time Yankee Stadium rocked as if it were filled to capacity. Zachary stood his

ground, however, and although Ruth cracked consecutive singles and came around to score after each of them, he was still one home run shy of his own record.

With the score tied 2–2, one out, and Koenig on third with a triple, Ruth came to bat in the eighth. He took Zachary's first pitch for a ball. The next pitch was a strike. The stadium crowd had left an indelible impression on the Washington pitcher: if Zachary's heart was void of charity, his arsenal of pitches showed not a trace of a base-on-balls. Ruth cocked his bat and waited for the one-one pitch. Zachary delivered and the Babe stroked it. The ball hugged the right field foul line all the way. It seemed to hang above the field. And then it disappeared, just a few feet fair, into the right field stands. The relentless Zachary rushed the umpire, screaming that the ball was foul, but Ruth circled the bases and there was bedlam in the Bronx. New York's Herb Pennock, in his final World Series tuneup, retired Washington in order in the ninth. The next day, writing in the New York *Daily Mirror,* Charles Segar described the game's final out.

> The final big thrill came as the Babe started for the dugout after catching Walter Johnson's fly in the ninth. Fans scaled the bleacher screen and ran after the Babe; they came from the boxes and the grandstand. And as the Babe was wending his way to the dugout, those persons, among them millionaires and newsboys, slapped him on the back. And the Babe liked it.

Ruth's historic 60th homer was retrieved in the bleachers by one Joe Forner, who ran to the Yankee clubhouse following the game to present it to the Babe. There, Ruth and his teammates were beside themselves in celebra-

Wherever you looked in the 1920s—and some places you wouldn't look—there was always the Babe.

tion. "Sixty, count'em, sixty!" said the Babe. "Let's see some other son of a bitch match that!"

That was 1927, and you can still find the number 60 in the record books under *Ruth, George Herman,* to the right of the year 1927 and in the column marked *HR.* The number stands like a monument to sluggers of all times, and in a game in which there is so much that is magical in so many numbers—300 wins in a career, 20 wins in a season, 27 consecutive outs to a perfect game, a .300 batting average—Ruth's number 60 may be the most magical of all. Despite Roger Maris' 61-homer season in 1961, it is Ruth's 60 that remains as the standard of achievement.

But like so many of Ruth's personal statistics, which were phenomenal— his 714 lifetime homers, his .342 batting average, his career record .690 slugging average—the real value of his 60th home run is not just in the number alone. The Yankees won that game 4–2, and the Babe's record-breaking homer once more provided the margin of victory. In the history of baseball, no one man ever did more in the cause of victory. In 163 appearances as a pitcher, Ruth won 94 games, lost only 46, and posted a 2.28 career ERA. In 1916 he won 23 games and led the league with a 1.75 ERA for the world champion Red Sox. The next year he won 24. In his 22-year career he played on ten pennant-winning teams and seven world champions. In addition to 15 World Series homers, a .326 Series average, and a .744 slugging percentage, Ruth won three games, lost none and pitched $29\frac{2}{3}$ consecutive scoreless innings, a Series record that lasted until Yankee lefthander Whitey Ford broke it in 1961. Perhaps the truest testimony to Ruth's greatness is how well his numbers have stood up over the years. In all of sports, there are no other instances

The Babe's popularity with kids was legendary, the stuff myths are made of. He turned generations of Americans into fans of the game he loved.

The Babe enjoyed a banner year in 1923 (opposite): Yankee Stadium opened; Ruth batted .393 with a league-leading 41 homers and was voted Most Valuable Player. The Yankees won their first World Series, defeating the Giants four games to two.

Ruth's hitting and pitching led the Boston Red Sox to world championships in 1916 and 1918. They haven't won another since.

In 1922, Ruth's Yankees outdrew John McGraw's Giants at the Polo Grounds, where both played home games. The next year, owner Jacob Ruppert opened Yankee Stadium.

of an athlete born nearly a century ago whose performances so outdistance those of so many of his modern counterparts. Ruth was the one magnificent exception.

No man who ever held a bat in his hands was as feared as Ruth. He was unstoppable. Nothing worked against him. Not overshifts, not intentional walks. Though he was primarily a pull hitter, he had exceptional power to the opposite field. Ruth probably got more bad pitches than anyone. According to Hall of Famer Joe Sewell, who played on Ruth's Yankees from 1931 to 1933, "The standing rule was that in the late innings, if Ruth came to bat and he could beat you, you walk him. No ifs, ands or buts." Only Ted Williams outranks Ruth in base-on-ball percentage, but Williams never willingly swung at bad balls. Had Ruth waited for good pitches, his bat would have been covered with cobwebs. The great Walter Johnson doubted if Ruth had any ". . . real batting weakness. He can hit any kind of ball that ever came within his reach hard enough to split the cover." It was startling to see how often he hit the ball out of the park on pitches far outside the strike zone: down around his shoelaces, up near the brim of his cap, a foot outside the plate. And he still set the single season record for walks: 170 in 1923, a record that still stands.

Long before Mickey Mantle "invented" the tape measure homer, Ruth was master of the long-distance call. No one before or since could hit a ball—often a "dead ball"—as far as the Babe. On April 4, 1919, while playing for the Red Sox in an exhibition game against the Giants on a makeshift field at a racetrack in Tampa, Florida, Ruth drove a ball that sportswriters estimated to have carried 612 feet. On June 8, 1926, Ruth propelled a rising line drive over the back wall of the right center field bleachers of Detroit's Navin Field. The ball carried completely over the wide breadth of Trumbull Avenue and came

By 1932, Hack Wilson (left)—whose 56 home runs as a Cub in 1930 came closer to Ruth's record than any National Leaguer ever—was a Brooklyn Dodger.

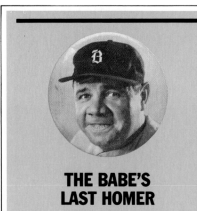

THE BABE'S LAST HOMER

There were no called shots, no promises to keep. In fact, until he announced his retirement eight days later, no one knew that May 25, 1935, was Babe Ruth's last day as a slugger.

Ruth was only 40, but drink and carousing had aged him beyond his years. And he was no longer a Yankee. Although he had hit .288 with 22 home runs for New York in 1934, the Yankees traded the Babe to the NL Boston Braves the following season. Ruth managed only six homers in '35, but three of them came on May 25 and were as memorable as any he hit.

"I guess it was a fastball," said Red Lucas, the Pirate right hander who served up Ruth's first. "I got it inside. I didn't want him to hit it back through the box at me."

The next two were off Guy Bush, Babe's nemesis from the 1932 World Series. "I told Tommy Padden, our catcher, 'I'm gonna throw the ball by this big monkey,'" Bush recalled. But Ruth lofted one into the short right field seats. "Is that the kind of home runs that big jackass been hitting in the American League?" Bush jeered.

Bush next challenged Ruth with a fastball, but got it up. "He hit it out of the cockeyed park! Looked like it went to St. Louis," Bush said.

"I watched him all around the bases. He just hobbled around, couldn't hardly run. As he went around third base, I took my cap off and bowed to him. He just kind of nodded and smiled."

Ruth went hitless in his next 5 games, and on June 2, the Braves gave him his unconditional release.

to earth far up on Plum Street, a distance of some 620 feet. And Sewell recalls one exhibition game when he scored "not once but twice from second base on sacrifice flies hit by Ruth—*that's* how far he hit 'em."

Ruth was 32 years old when he broke the record in 1927. He was in his 14th big league season and was hitting .350 for his career. His 416 home runs were light years ahead of anyone else. And though he still had eight years and nearly 300 homers left in his bat, his career was on the downslide. His body had already begun to assume the top-heavy shape that would identify him for the rest of his life and forever. The grossest aspects of the many legends that surrounded the life of the man–the drinking, gluttony, and womanizing—had begun to consume the body of the athlete. By 1927, he had begun to look very much the persona whose image is indelibly stamped into the minds of the millions who never saw him play—the fat playboy of Prohibition.

Given the uncountable myths that surrounded Ruth and the unlikely, unathletic manner—the spindly legs, the huge upper torso, the slightly stooped posture—that seemed to feed those myths, there's little wonder that an appreciation of Ruth's greatness has begun to slip from the grasp of the modern fan. In his day, Babe Ruth was not only the most popular man in the country, he was a fearsome athlete. At 6'2" and 215 pounds, Ruth was graceful, strong and fast. In his first two years with the Yankees Ruth stole 31 bases. As a former pitcher with Hall of Fame potential, Ruth's arm in the outfield was accurate and near ballistic in speed.

In the 1920s, the only thing equal to Ruth's athletic prowess was his spirit. Amid the terrible disillusionment that swept the country following the fixing

George Herman Ruth (far right) signed his first professional contract in 1913 at the age of 18 with the minor league Baltimore Orioles (above).

of the 1919 World Series, the "Black Sox Scandal," Ruth almost single-handedly restored America's wonderment in its national pastime, which he did in the largest, most dramatic way available to him—the home run. Ruth did not invent the homer, though his name and the home run continue to remain virtually synonymous. But the frequency with which he cleared the bases with a single blast—and the joy fans derived from watching him perform—made the homer the most potent weapon in the game, even as we know it today. He seemed capable of hitting home runs at will and is said to have delivered on promised homers time and again.

In the 1932 World Series against the Chicago Cubs, Ruth is said to have "called his shot" against Cub pitcher Charley Root. After acknowledging the first two strikes by holding up one, then two, fingers, Ruth pointed with an assured vengeance in the direction the center field bleachers of Wrigley Field. Then he golfed the very next pitch, a two-two curve, precisely where he had pointed. Then he roared in laughter as he circled the bases.

Like many great stories about Ruth, his "called" World Series homer may or may not be apocryphal. To this day it remains unclear whether he actually pointed or whether his gesture was directed at Root. Whatever the truth, one thing is irrefutable: the almost childlike pleasure Ruth derived from that home run was apparent whenever he came to bat. Although he was an incurable heckler of opposing players, the joy he brought to the field—win or lose—was infectious, among teammates, opposition, and fans throughout the country. It was a happiness ingrained in him as he learned the game as a boy in Baltimore. The irrepressible son of a Baltimore saloon keeper, Ruth held fast to his youthful feeling for the game throughout his professional baseball career. By the time he was sold by Red Sox owner Harry Frazee to Jacob

Sixteen months before his death on August 16, 1948, Ruth stood at the plate in Yankee Stadium for the last time.

Ruppert and the Yankees on January 3, 1920, there were already designs on the Babe's growing popularity, which the Yankees ultimately exploited to the fullest.

And not even the wild baseball promotions of recent years can match the extent to which the Yankee front office was capable of selling Ruth to the public. The Yankees scheduled exhibition games and all sorts of promotional functions and ceremonies designed around the Babe. In an era when the most expedient form of travel was by rail, Ruth and the Yankees journeyed to cities and towns as distant as Columbus, Ohio, and Albany on "off-days" where thousands of people were happy to pay for the chance to see the legend perform. Long before ballplayers employed agents—though he surely could have put dozens to work—Babe Ruth was the first superstar of sport. His combined earnings, on and off the field, were in the millions. And by 1930 he was earning the unheard of salary of $80,000 a year as a ballplayer.

But Ruth was more than a superstar, more than what we know that term to mean today. Ruth was a folk hero—"The Sultan of Swat"—and folk heroes last. Ask *anyone* of any age to name a famous athlete and odds are he'll name Babe Ruth. Ruth's hero's role was one he welcomed and consciously honored even to his final appearance at Yankee Stadium, The House That Ruth Built, on April 27, 1947. With only 16 months to live, his body lean and bowed from cancer, Ruth addressed the 60,000 people present. His voice was weak and raspy, and he spoke briefly into the microphone at homeplate. "You know," he said, "the only real game in the world, I think, is baseball." ◗

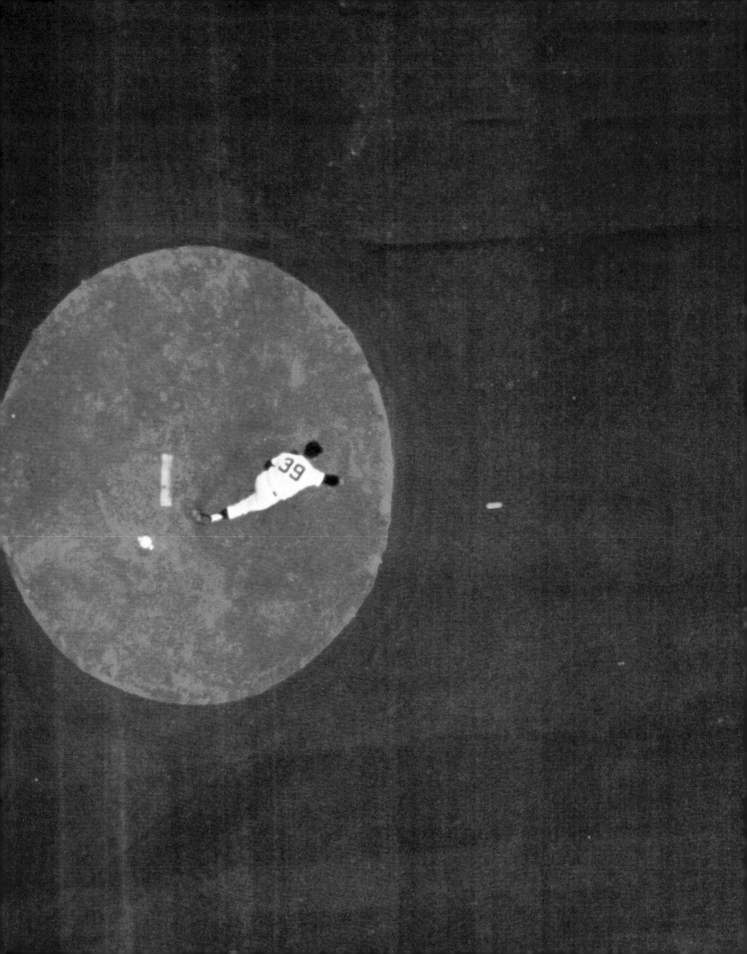

How Hard Is Hitting?

You ever walk into a pitch-black room full of furniture that you've never seen before and try to walk through it without bumping into anything? Well, it's harder than that.

Ted Kluszewski

Chicago White Sox second baseman Nellie Fox (2) greeted Ted Williams after the Boston slugger homered in the 1956 All-Star Game. Mickey Mantle (7) followed with another home run off Milwaukee's Warren Spahn, but the National League countered with homers from Stan Musial and Willie Mays for a 7–3 win.

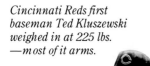

Cincinnati Reds first baseman Ted Kluszewski weighed in at 225 lbs. —most of it arms.

When Ted Williams offered advice, pitchers as well as hitters listened. Even Warren Spahn, the winningest left-handed pitcher in history, listened. "That's a pretty good fastball," Williams smiled. "You ought to use it more often." "That's strange," answered Spahn. "I always thought my curve was my best pitch."

That was in 1956, during a meaningless spring training game. The two didn't meet again until the All-Star Game in Washington that summer. The National League was ahead 4–0, and Spahn, in relief of Pittsburgh's Bob Friend, had held the American League scoreless for two innings, when Williams came up with a man on first in the bottom of the sixth. As he looked in for the sign, Spahn's mind drifted back to that early spring afternoon in Florida. "Now's the time to give him the fastball," he told himself.

Williams was waiting. He drove Spahn's fastball into the center field bullpen. "You conned me into that pitch, didn't you?" Spahn demanded as Williams rounded second. Williams only smiled and kept on jogging.

The Williams-Spahn duel, what Williams liked to call "the little hitter-pitcher thinking game," lies at the heart of baseball. In a war of countless casualties, the batter is so much at the mercy of the pitcher that he can fail seven out of ten times and still be considered successful. "The pitcher can win the battles," says New York Yankee slugger Dave Winfield, "the batter can win the war." But never as often as he would like.

Consider what happens as a batter steps up to the plate, facing a pitcher like Nolan Ryan, glaring down from a small hill 20 yards away. Ryan releases his fastball—five ounces of power clocked at 90 miles per hour. It reaches home plate .45 seconds later. To turn that pitch into a home run, the batter, in

New York Yankee third baseman Graig Nettles demonstrates the lengths to which sluggers must go to generate power. Nettles' swing was tailor-made to Yankee Stadium's short right field fence.

Hank Aaron's powerful wrists—strengthened in his youth by lugging blocks of ice—allowed him to wait longer before starting his swing than most power hitters. Ted Williams called Aaron "one of baseball's smartest hitters."

Fourteen players hit more homers in their careers than Pittsburgh's Willie Stargell, but only one—Reggie Jackson—struck out more.

the blink of an eye, has to whip the sweet part of the bat against the ball, stop its momentum completely, and redirect all that speeding energy back into the sky at an acute angle toward a fence 300 to 400 feet away.

The anatomy of a major league home run is really a study in time. According to Spahn, "Hitting is timing. Pitching is upsetting timing." Here's how 1988 major league home run champ José Canseco deals with the little time his rival —say, Boston's Roger Clemens or Minnesota's Frank Viola—is willing to allow him.

In approximately .13 seconds, the first 18 feet, Canseco sights the ball— "picks it up," in players' parlance—spots its rotation, predicts its speed and direction, and makes a go/no-go decision to take, swing or duck and run. At .28 seconds—about 37 feet—Canseco whips the bat around to the exact spot where he thinks the curving, rising, hopping or sinking ball will be, timing the swing for the precise moment it will be there. If Canseco puts the sweet spot of the bat—an area about four inches long—on the dead center of the ball, he will smack a line drive toward center field. For a homer, he needs to hit the ball an eighth of an inch below the center, in order to give it height and back-spin. A quarter-inch too high or too low, .03 seconds too early or too late, and he has to settle for a foul ball, a pop-up, a ground out, or even a complete miss. Roger Maris said that in 1962, the year after he hit his record 61 home runs, he was meeting the ball an eighth of an inch higher and hitting line drive doubles instead of lofting fly ball homers.

Whatever the speed of the pitch, from 75 to nearly 100 miles per hour, the ball literally moves too fast for the batter to follow its path to the plate. Ted Williams' eyesight and bat speed allowed him to wait an additional .03 seconds, or four feet, before he swung. "Hitting it out of the catcher's mitt,"

Stan Musial was a big-time slugger with the bat control of a contact hitter. From 1941 to 1963 Musial hit 30 or more homers six times, won seven batting titles, and averaged just 33 strikeouts per season.

From 1967 to 1970, Washington's Frank Howard hit more homers—172—than anyone in baseball. From May 12 to 18, 1968, Howard hit more homers—10—than anyone ever has in one week.

Williams called it. But even Williams doubts that he ever saw ball meeting bat. "I've seen what I thought was the ball going over my bat—I think." Hank Aaron is one of the few players who claim to have seen the bat hit the ball.

At the speeds with which major league pitches travel, it's not surprising that sight, of all the senses, is so rarely recalled when players talk about great slugging feats. If that's so, what does a hitter look for when he steps up to the plate? Should he guess what pitch is about to come his way? Of course, says Williams. He knew that pitchers knew he could hit a fastball, so he always guessed curve—until the slider came into the league and complicated the odds of guessing correctly. Aaron, on the other hand, guessed fastball and adjusted to the curve. Joe Sewell says that he looked only for the pitch to be in the strike zone. "If your swing is level," claims Sewell, "you'll get your hits." Reggie Jackson says that it's "calculated anticipation" based on everything the hitter knows about the pitcher and the situation. Ex-Pirate Hall of Famer Willie Stargell studied the man who calls the signals, saying that he hit more off the catcher than the pitcher.

According to Sewell, "Most players just don't know how to talk about hitting." But on one thing most hitters will agree: consciously trying for a home run is a good way to make an out. Hank Aaron says that 90 percent of his home runs came when he wasn't thinking homer. "You think home run, you overswing," warns Frank Robinson, who played from 1968 to 1971 under Baltimore manager Earl Weaver, a proponent of the big inning. Whether or not Weaver ever ordered Robinson to "think homer" isn't the point; in the late innings of a tight game, a power hitter like Robinson is *expected* to homer.

Stan Musial, the great Cardinal slugger who batted .331 with 475 home runs, once decided to improve his slugging prowess—and paid for it. "The

Frank Robinson's tremendous upper body strength and intimidating presence allowed him to crowd the plate as few players ever have. Robinson (opposite) played on one pennant winner during his 1956–65 stint with the Cincinnati Reds, and on four more in his six years with the Baltimore Orioles.

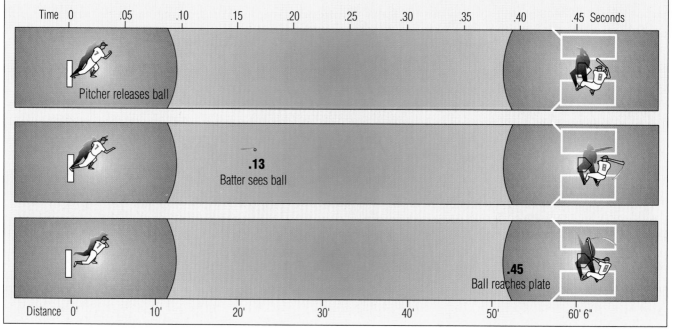

Timing the Pitch

The decision of a batter to swing or to take a pitch is one of sport's most underestimated athletic skills. It is also one of the most instinctive. For a major league batter facing a 90 mile-per-hour fastball, the moment of truth comes in less than half a second.

Time   0   .05   .10   .15   .20   .25   .30   .35   .40   .45 Seconds

Pitcher releases ball

.13
Batter sees ball

.45
Ball reaches plate

Distance   0'   10'   20'   30'   40'   50'   60' 6"

best year I ever had was in '48. I hit .376 and had 39 home runs. I got to thinking about it that winter and came to the dumbest decision I ever made in my life.

" 'You hit 39 homers last season,' I said to myself, 'and every one was an accident. If you ever concentrated on homers, who knows, maybe you'd be up there with Babe Ruth.' So I started swinging from my heels as soon as the season began." At the All-Star break, Musial was hitting a mere .300 with only 15 home runs. " 'The hell with the homers,' I said to myself. 'Let's start getting some base hits.' When the season ended, I had 36 homers and a .338 batting average. I never went deliberately after a home run again."

How, then, does it feel to hit a home run into the bleachers of a major league ballpark? What is the feeling, the sensation in your hands, your arms, your body? Frank Robinson, whose 586 career home runs rank fourth on the all-time list, says, "You don't feel anything. You don't even feel it when it hits the bat, but you know it when it makes contact. You *know* it. You know you've done everything right."

Even Wade Boggs, the most committed student of hitting since Williams, says that he knows when he has hit a ball well by a "feeling" he gets. A feeling! "When you *don't* hit the ball good," says 6'7" Frank Howard, "you feel it." Who hasn't experienced what Howard is talking about, the failure to get "good wood" on the ball? A hit off the fists on a cold March afternoon; a fastball in on the handle when you've loosened your grip on the bat. A bat is like a guitar string—it resonates when struck. But there is one spot where there is no resonance, the "sweet zone," where batters feel no vibration at all.

Yankee first baseman Don Mattingly claims to have smelled burning

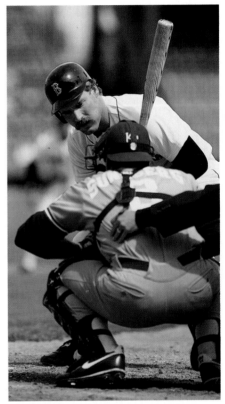

Jimmie Foxx cut an awesome figure at the plate. Broad shouldered and exceptionally strong, he hit some of the longest home runs ever. Foxx led the Athletics to pennants in 1929, 1930 and 1931, then was sold to Boston in 1936, where his power made a lasting impression on a kid named Ted Williams.

Concentration is the key to Boston third baseman Wade Boggs' startling success at the plate. A contact hitter, Boggs was asked in 1987 to hit more home runs. He responded with 24 homers—three times his previous high—and still his average rose six points to .363.

wood on two or three occasions after having made contact. Oddly enough, those moments were not when Mattingly hammered a fastball into the third deck of Yankee Stadium, but when he just *missed* hammering one. Williams claims that he, too, at least three times, could actually smell wood burning. Williams, who apparently knows as much about physics as he does about hitting—and pitching and fishing—says that when bat and ball meet, the seams of the ball can generate enough friction against the wood to induce the slightest amount of scorching.

In 20 years in the majors, Jimmie Foxx, who teamed with Ted Williams on the Red Sox from 1939 through 1942, hit 534 career home runs. Asked about a "Double X" round tripper, Williams didn't describe it in terms of distance and height. He remembered the sound. When pressed, he could only liken the sound of a Foxx homer to one by Mickey Mantle. The *sound* of their homers was that unique. Joe Sewell, a Hall of Fame shortstop who played both with and against Babe Ruth for 14 seasons, says that "when Ruth'd hit those homers you'd hear that echo in the stadium—it sounded like a pistol shootin'."

Even more than his bat, a slugger's stance is his identification card. Hall of Famer Al Simmons earned his nickname "Bucketfoot" by putting his front foot "in the bucket"—that is, stepping far away from the plate and down the third base line. Negro League home run king Norman "Turkey" Stearnes waited with his front heel down and his toe pointed skyward. Two all-time greats, Rogers Hornsby and Roberto Clemente, stood deep in the batter's box and stepped toward the plate. Jimmie Foxx and Mickey Mantle took long strides; Joe DiMaggio hardly strode at all; Mel Ott kicked up his right leg, as did Sadaharu Oh, the Japanese home run king.

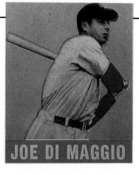

JOE DI MAGGIO

Joe DiMaggio—The Streak

It was known simply as "The Streak."
Like Charles Lindbergh's flight before it, Joe DiMaggio's consecutive-game hitting streak captured the imagination of a nation. A real-life daytime drama, DiMaggio's 56-game streak gave Americans something they desperately needed in 1941—a reason to cheer. With war in Europe and economic uncertainty at home, the streak put something hopeful and wondrous on the radio each day, if only briefly. And it catapulted a shy, self-conscious 26-year-old into the nation's spotlight and its psyche.

It started innocently enough, with a single in a 13–1 Yankee loss to the Chicago White Sox on May 15. Two years earlier DiMaggio had won the American League's Most Valuable Player Award and played on his fourth world championship team in as many years. But the Yanks had slipped to third in 1940, fourth by mid-May of 1941. DiMaggio had hit just .237 in his last 13 games, and a May 16 headline in the *Journal-American* pronounced "Yank Attack Weakest in Years." The streak got no press at all until it reached 18, and DiMaggio said he didn't notice it until he hit 24 and writers began to research hitting streak records.

DiMaggio adjusted his stance in late May, and by June he and the Yankees were in a groove. He broke the Yankee record of 29 straight with help from a bad-hop grounder that hit White Sox shortstop Luke Appling in the shoulder. The streak so inspired St. Louis Browns pitcher Bob Muncrief

that he disobeyed orders to walk DiMaggio—then hitless—in the eighth inning of game 36. DiMaggio singled to keep the streak alive. "I wasn't going to walk him," Muncrief said. "That wouldn't have been fair to him or me. Heck, he's the greatest player I ever saw."

In game 38, DiMaggio was hitless going into the bottom of the eighth with the Yankees leading 3–1. With one out, Red Rolfe on first, and DiMaggio on deck, Tommy Henrich grabbed a bat. Henrich asked Yankee manager Joe McCarthy if he could drop a sacrifice bunt to avoid the double play, and McCarthy agreed. Once again DiMaggio benefited from a pitcher's nobility, this time St. Louis' Eldon Auker. With first base open, Auker pitched to DiMaggio, who doubled to left. "Auker's a big man, he won't walk him," Henrich remembered thinking.

Nobility was noticeably absent in game 40 as DiMaggio faced Philadelphia's Johnny Babich, who had crippled the Yankees the year before, beating them five times. After retiring DiMaggio his first time up, Babich threw him three straight balls way off the plate. "He was out to stop me," DiMaggio said, "even if it meant walking me every time up." Babich threw another pitch nowhere near the strike zone, but DiMaggio, given the green light, smashed a line drive through Babich's legs into center for a double and sweet revenge. "When I got to second base and looked at Babich, he was white as a ghost," DiMaggio said.

DiMaggio tied George Sisler's American

JOE DiMAGGIO

Outfield
New York Yankees 1936–1942,
    1946–1951
Hall of Fame 1955

GAMES	**1,736**
AT BATS	**6,821**
BATTING AVERAGE	
Career	**.325**
Season High	**.381**
BATTING TITLES	**1939, 1940**
SLUGGING AVERAGE	
Career *(6th all time)*	**.579**
Season High	**.673**
HITS	
Career	**2,214**
Season High	**215**
DOUBLES	
Career	**389**
Season High	**44**
TRIPLES	
Career	**131**
Season High	**15**
HOME RUNS	
Career	**361**
Season High	**46**
TOTAL BASES	**3,948**
EXTRA BASE HITS	**881**
RUNS BATTED IN	
Career	**1,537**
Season High	**167**
RUNS	
Career	**1,390**
Season High	**151**
WORLD SERIES	**1936-1939**
1941, 1942, 1947, 1949-1951	
MOST VALUABLE PLAYER	
1939,1941,1947	

League record of 41 straight in the first game of a doubleheader against Washington, but between games someone stole DiMaggio's bat, which he had worked over with a soupbone and rubbed with olive oil and resin. After going hitless in the nightcap until the seventh, he retrieved a bat he had loaned to Henrich and singled. The stolen bat was returned a few days later.

On July 2 DiMaggio homered to break Wee Willie Keeler's major league mark of 44. Twelve games later, Cleveland third baseman Ken Keltner robbed DiMaggio twice and Lou Boudreau snagged his bad-hop grounder in the eighth inning to end the streak at 56 games. The next day DiMaggio started another streak that lasted 17 games.

Boston's Ted Williams actually outhit DiMaggio during those 56 games—.412 to .408—but it was the Yankees who won the pennant and DiMaggio who won the MVP and the hearts of millions. The introverted DiMaggio became a national hero, was immortalized in song by Paul Simon and in story by Ernest Hemingway, and married America's most glamorous woman—Marilyn Monroe.

During their honeymoon in 1954, Monroe left DiMaggio briefly to appear before 100,000 American servicemen in Korea. When she returned she told him, "It was wonderful, Joe. You never heard such cheering."

"Yes, I have," he said.

DiMaggio got three hits—including this single—July 16, 1941, against the Cleveland Indians, but his streak ended the next day.

For any hitter—from Rod Carew, who was known as the man of a thousand stances, to Marv Throneberry of the Mets, whose stance, though never his stats, mirrored Mickey Mantle's—the stance is what becomes the swing. Today, most of these batting-stance idiosyncrasies appear to have gone the way of chewing tobacco and Ebbetts Field. It would appear that they've been replaced by two or three basic stances. Perhaps those old styles that served yesterday's heroes so well just won't work against today's hurlers—Mike Scott's forkball or Tom Seaver's burner. Who's to say?

Movies of Babe Ruth show a man breaking most of the rules. He had a pronounced "hitch" in his swing, bringing his bat handle down to his waist. And, from a feet-together stance, he took a big stride into the ball. Sometimes, Ruth even took a couple of steps.

As hard as it is to belt a ball into the stands, there's usually no question about it once the ball leaves the bat. No statement is as self-assured as the remark "I knew it was gone the moment I hit it." As fans, we've come to expect this "understanding" from major leaguers. Whether it's true or not, nothing in modern baseball reinforces the claim as much as the "home run trot," a stylistic gesture that, to the uninitiated—or the insecure pitcher—suggests that the batter actually expected to clobber it all along, that he "knew what was coming."

Although the swagger of the home run trot might seem to be a phenomenon of the 1980s, it's really nothing more than another little hitter-pitcher game. The slugger who stands at the plate, watches the ball arc into the grandstand, and then starts down the baseline demonstrates a remarkable presence of mind, not to mention a good dose of ego.

Throughout his career, Babe Ruth looked almost comical in his mincing

The best power-hitting switch hitter since Mickey Mantle, first baseman Eddie Murray has hit some of the highest, hardest home runs in Baltimore Orioles history.

The Polo Grounds

When John B. Day brought professional baseball to New York in 1880, he arranged to use the Polo Grounds between Fifth and Sixth avenues and bounded by 110th and 112th streets. The field had been previously used by the Westchester Polo Association.

When the grandstand was torn down by the city in 1889 to complete Douglas Circle, the New York legislature passed a bill turning Manhattan Field, at 155th Street and Eighth Avenue, into a baseball park. On July 8, 1889, the Giants were in their new park on a small parcel of land along the Harlem River known as Coogan's Hollow, which fans continued to call the Polo Grounds. Despite the name, the new field was never the site of a polo match.

In 1902 John McGraw came to New York as the Giants' manager and built a team that dominated baseball for 20 years. But on April 14, 1911, a fire destroyed the Polo Grounds' wooden grandstand. The next morning Giants owner John T. Brush pledged to build "the finest [stadium] that can be constructed." With the Giants homeless for more than two months, the American League's Highlanders graciously allowed them to play home games at Hilltop Park.

The Giants' new park opened with a capacity of 16,000 on June 28. The steel and concrete stadium was a double-decked horseshoe where fans actually walked down to enter the upper tier. By the 1911 World Series between the Giants and the Philadelphia Athletics, seating capacity had increased to 34,000. Two years later, Brush returned the Highlanders' favor, letting them play home games in the Polo Grounds. By 1921, the tenants, now known as the Yankees—and home run king Babe Ruth—were outdrawing the landlord Giants. Following the Giants' World Series victory over the Yankees in 1921, McGraw terminated his tenant's lease. In 1923, with the Yankees in the comfort of a 70,000-seat palace across the Harlem River and within sight of fans in the Polo Grounds' upper deck, Brush increased the seating capacity of the Polo Grounds to 56,000.

The Polo Grounds was a home run paradise, where a fly ball down either line could produce dramatic results. Bobby Thomson's pennant-winning "shot heard round the world" off the Dodgers' Ralph Branca in the 1951 National League playoffs is a perfect example. But it also could be a slugger's nightmare, as Cleveland's Vic Wertz learned when Willie Mays corralled his 450-foot drive to center in the first game of the 1954 World Series.

As unkind as the Polo Grounds was to fastball pitchers—the foul lines measured just 258 feet to right, only 250 feet to the upper deck in left, and 279 to the lower deck—the monstrous center field, which generally measured 483 feet from home plate, allowed pitchers ample margin for error. Christy Mathewson's fadeaway and Carl Hubbell's screwball enabled these Giants' pitchers to enjoy remarkable success in the big park.

The memories that the Polo Grounds evoke are timeless: the moon rising over the center field scoreboard as night games unfolded; the Eddie Grant Memorial, honoring a fallen Giant veteran from World War I, below the clubhouses in center; Joe DiMaggio catching the final out in Game 2 of the 1936 World Series and ascending the clubhouse steps without breaking stride; the "hapless" Mets' first season. It's unlikely any park ever captured so many monumental moments as the horseshoe below Coogan's Bluff.

The Polo Grounds through the years: (clockwise from top left) the 1911 World Series; in 1962 as home to the expansion Mets; with fans waiting all night for tickets to Game 1 of the 1922 World Series.

The Polo Grounds

159th Street and Eighth Avenue
New York, New York

Built 1891
Rebuilt 1911
Demolished 1964

New York Giants, NL 1891-1957
New York Yankees, AL 1913-1922
New York Mets, NL 1962-1963

Seating Capacity 55,000

Style
Grass surface, asymmetrical, steel and concrete

Height of Outfield Fences
Left field foul pole: 17 feet
Left center field: 18 feet
Dead center field: 80 feet
Right center field: 12 feet
Right field foul pole: 11 feet

Dugouts
Home: 1st base
Visitors: 3rd base

Bullpens
Outfield, fair territory
Home: right center
Visitors: left center

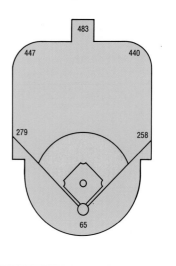

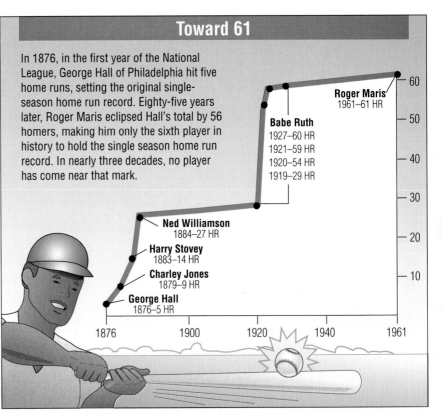

Toward 61

In 1876, in the first year of the National League, George Hall of Philadelphia hit five home runs, setting the original single-season home run record. Eighty-five years later, Roger Maris eclipsed Hall's total by 56 homers, making him only the sixth player in history to hold the single season home run record. In nearly three decades, no player has come near that mark.

Roger Maris
1961–61 HR

Babe Ruth
1927–60 HR
1921–59 HR
1920–54 HR
1919–29 HR

Ned Williamson
1884–27 HR

Harry Stovey
1883–14 HR

Charley Jones
1879–9 HR

George Hall
1876–5 HR

1876   1900   1920   1940   1961

60
50
40
30
20
10

Both Sadaharu Oh (above) and Mel Ott (right) used high leg kicks to generate power—Oh as Japan's all-time home run king, Ott as a Hall of Fame outfielder with the New York Giants from 1926 to 1946.

Hitting guru Charlie Lau called Boston's Carl Yastrzemski (above) "possibly the hardest working hitter I've ever seen." As he got older, Yastrzemski's willingness to change his stance made him one of just four players with 400 homers and 3,000 hits.

Mets right fielder Darryl Strawberry answers pitchers' windups with one of his own—a stylized, 1980s version of Ott's leg kick. Strawberry curls his bat behind his head, then explodes into the pitch, generating tremendous power and a lot of strikeouts.

little steps as he rounded the bases following a home run, acknowledging the crowd with a brief tip-of-the-cap. Ted Williams never tipped his cap to anyone. In each of his 521 career homers, Williams was totally businesslike, rounding the bases in a quick, loping stride with his head bowed, much like Mickey Mantle, his rival in the 1950s. But whereas Williams seemed to look down out of deference to his act, Mantle seemed to lower his head in the pained expression his body wore as he ran—elbows and forearms tucked to his sides and pumping, while his legs churned gingerly.

It's hard to say who, if anyone, truly invented the home run trot, though no one performed it any better than did Reggie Jackson following his third consecutive home run against the Dodgers in Game 6 of the 1977 World Series. The *way* the player runs the bases seems as vital in the 1980s as the home run itself. Jose Canseco, Darryl Strawberry, Eddie Murray—each one, to a certain degree, possesses a touch of swagger in his home run trot. Like most things in baseball, it's more than style and it's surely connected in the player's mind with his individual way of hitting—his stance. If you watch some players carefully enough, you can see how the home run trot is an extension—or, in some cases, an exaggeration—of his stance. Reggie Jackson is the perfect case in point.

How hard is hitting? Williams is famous for having said that "hitting a baseball is the single most difficult thing to do in all of sport," as controversial a statement as ever was made. How odd that, in a game played for more than a century by the same rules and boundaries, so few are capable of doing what they want to do most.

Apparently, it's the *desire* of hitters, more than anything else, that has

Absolutely Lau

Charlie Lau was not the first hitting coach in history, only the first to identify the elements necessary to hit a baseball successfully. The "absolutes of hitting," Lau called them, and he instructed his pupils accordingly. Even non-believer Ted Williams, say Lau and disciple Walt Hriniak, followed the Lau method.

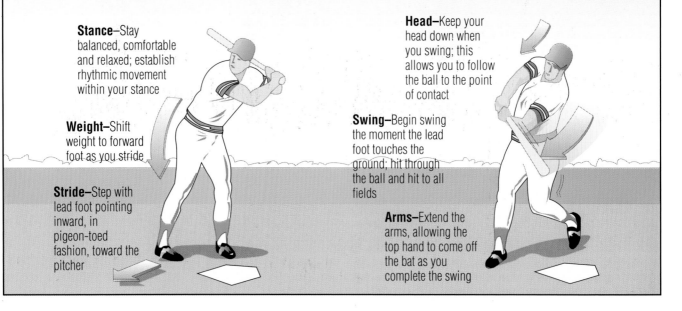

Stance–Stay balanced, comfortable and relaxed; establish rhythmic movement within your stance

Weight–Shift weight to forward foot as you stride

Stride–Step with lead foot pointing inward, in pigeon-toed fashion, toward the pitcher

Head–Keep your head down when you swing; this allows you to follow the ball to the point of contact

Swing–Begin swing the moment the lead foot touches the ground; hit through the ball and hit to all fields

Arms–Extend the arms, allowing the top hand to come off the bat as you complete the swing

The only thing ballplayers do more than hit is talk about hitting. Former Red Sox batting coach Walt Hriniak (at left) and veteran outfielder Dave Henderson are of like minds on the subject.

changed the most over the years. Hitting coach Lee May says that today's hitters are more scientific than ever before. May cites the use of computers, the availability of pitching machines and batting tees, the use of video tapes, and the specialization of hitting instructors as reasons for the apparent homogeneity of hitting styles. Actually, more than 60 years ago Joe Sewell was saying the same thing, though Sewell said it more simply: "Hitting is scientific —if you do it right, you're sure to hit the ball."

In the 1980s, the "right" way for many hitters appears to be the Charlie Lau way. According to Lau, the *real* challenge, the thing that can keep ball-players awake nights, is to hit the ball *consistently*—day after day, in game after game throughout the season. The Lau theory plays down going for the home run, because doing so cancels consistency. Practicing the Lau technique properly becomes an all-or-nothing proposition.

Curiously, the two high priests of batting —Walt Hriniak, who professed the Lau theory, and Ted Williams—both worked for the same boss, the Boston Red Sox. Boston's management saw no contradiction in inviting Williams to work with rookies every March, then giving Hriniak a free hand to un-teach most of those lessons over the next six months. Of course, Boston's minor league coaches don't teach Hriniak's methods, either. The main points of disagreement concern the timing and movement of the hips and hands, the arc and plane of the swing, and the distribution of the batter's weight.

The players themselves variously follow one or the other of these masters. In 1968, Reggie Jackson found that he "was getting [his] hips in the way"—that is, he was not turning them fast enough. So he concentrated on turning them sooner. The next year he hit 47 home runs.

"I don't think you should put that much weight on your back leg," says

Atlanta center fielder Dale Murphy has hit more home runs than any Brave since Hank Aaron, yet the two couldn't be farther apart on their approach to hitting.

Yankee first baseman Don Mattingly has the sweetest swing—and stats—in the 1980s. His emphatic weight shift is key.

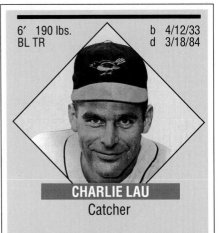

6′ 190 lbs.   b 4/12/33
BL TR   d 3/18/84

CHARLIE LAU
Catcher

A career .255 hitter with no power to speak of, Charlie Lau was traded four times, twice for cash. Then in the 1970s with the Kansas City Royals, Charlie Lau became a batting coach and all but revolutionized hitting.

Lau played just 527 games in 11 years but, like a lot of great coaches and managers, made good use of his time on the bench. Lau argued against always trying to hit home runs, and instead stressed good mechanics to make consistent contact. Power hitters are pull hitters, Lau said, and to pull the ball you've got to get the bat head out earlier, leaving almost no margin for error. Hitting home runs was an advanced technique to be mastered later.

Lau's theory of hitting involved a pronounced weight shift, a slightly downward swing, and release of the top hand for full extension. He produced a batch of line drive hitters who used the entire field, including two-time American League batting champ George Brett.

By 1976, Lau had helped turn the Royals from an also-ran expansion team to a division power. Led by Lau's disciples Brett, Hal McRae, Frank White, and Darrell Porter, the Royals won three straight division titles. Despite having mediocre team power, the Royals were consistently at or near the top of the league in runs scored.

Lau's enormous contribution to the game is visible in the swings of great hitters like Brett, Boston's Wade Boggs, and New York's Don Mattingly.

No one got more out of Charlie Lau's hitting technique than Kansas City third baseman George Brett, but then no one brought as much talent and intensity to the task. In 1980, Brett hit .390 —the best batting average in 39 years—and led the majors with a .664 slugging average.

Hank Aaron, presently director of player development of the Atlanta Braves. But Dale Murphy, who has hit well over 300 homers for the Braves, says, "I'm a back-foot swinger."

Three-time batting champ and Twins batting coach Tony Oliva says that 90 percent of the good hitters stay back. But Frank Robinson claims that the weight should be back and braced against the front foot.

In terms of home run production, critics of the Lau method say that Lau and Hriniak have created a breed of ping hitters. Old timers say that they've set hitting back 25 years. "What about Ron Kittle, Greg Luzinski, Dwight Evans, and George Brett?" Hriniak retorts. "Are they ping hitters?"

So the debate goes on.

A reporter once asked Babe Ruth what he tells people when they ask for the secret of hitting. "All I can tell 'em," the Babe answered sagely, "is I pick out a good one and I sock it." Which was pretty much the theory of Yogi Berra, baseball's resident guru for the past 40 years and one of the most notorious bad-ball hitters in history. Berra, so the story goes, was suffering a horrendous spring training early in his career when his manager advised him to "think when you go up to the plate." His next time up, Berra took three straight strikes. Returning to the dugout and a chewing out by the manager, Berra defended himself by asking, "How can you think and hit at the same time?"

Years later, when Berra was managing the Mets, a rookie came to him saying, "Mr. Berra, I've got this problem: I keep swinging up on the ball."

"Well," replied Berra, determined not to confuse the rookie, "swing down." How hard is hitting? It's *that* simple! ◗

Red Sox right fielder Dwight Evans demonstrates a classic follow-through from the Charlie Lau school of hitting. But Evans brings power to Lau's technique and, at the age of 36, hit a career-high 34 homers in 1987.

Hank Aaron

I t's easy to diminish Hank Aaron's achievements and assail the way he rewrote baseball's record books, and many have delighted in doing so. He hit 41 more home runs and had 86 more RBI than Babe Ruth, but it took almost 4,000 more at-bats for him to do it. Mays was a better outfielder and base runner, and Mantle had more sheer power. Besides, more than half of Aaron's home runs came after his Braves moved to Atlanta and the homer paradise of Fulton County Stadium.

But what Aaron did was more—more homers, more RBI, more total bases, more hitting than any player before or since. In many ways he was the most complete player of all time. Aaron's numbers are just plain bigger than anyone else's. He had thirteen .300-batting-average seasons, eleven 100-RBI seasons, fourteen 100-runs-scored seasons, and six 40-home-run seasons. He ranks first all-time in homers and RBI; second in at-bats; third in runs scored, games played, and hits; and eighth in doubles. He led the National League in homers, RBI, slugging percentage, and doubles four times each, and won two batting titles. He was an outstanding right fielder with a good arm and better speed—he stole 20 or more bases six times.

Aaron's no-nonsense approach to the game made him appear indifferent to some, but he played baseball to satisfy himself and his teammates, not the press. "I came to the Braves on business," he said, "and I intended to see that business was good as long as I could."

Aaron began his career at 16, hitting crosshanded for the Mobile Black Bears, a semi-professional team. Late in the 1951 season, he joined the Indianapolis Clowns of the National Negro League. In 1953 the Milwaukee Braves may have gotten the biggest bargain in the history of baseball when they bought Aaron's contract from the Clowns for $1,000. In return they got 23 years of workmanlike excellence. In 1954, at age 20, he joined an already power-laden Braves' lineup featuring Eddie Mathews and Joe Adcock. Milwaukee was a solid first division team, but when Aaron exploded for 44 homers and 132 RBI in 1957, he carried the Braves to their first pennant in Milwaukee —his eleventh-inning homer against the Cardinals clinched the flag on September 23. In the World Series, Aaron and pitcher Lew Burdette were a two-man gang as the Braves beat the Yankees in seven games. Burdette won three games—two of them shutouts—and Aaron hit .393 with three homers and seven RBI against a Yankee pitching staff that posted a 3.00 regular season ERA. Aaron had a World Series ring, a batting title, and a home run title, and he was just 24 years old.

Aaron helped the Braves to another pennant in 1958 and hit .333 in the Series, but the Yankees became the first team to win after being down three games to one. The Braves moved to Atlanta in 1966 and in 1969 won the first championship of the National League's new West Division. Despite a three-game playoff sweep by the New York Mets, Aaron again sparkled in postseason play, hitting .357 with three homers and seven RBI.

After his playing career ended and he joined the Braves' front office, Aaron became an outspoken critic of the shortage of blacks in top level field and front office positions. But while he played,

Aaron was a great student of pitchers and was at his best against the best. He hit more homers against Dodger ace Don Drysdale—17—than against any other pitcher.

HANK AARON

Outfield, First Base
Designated Hitter
Milwaukee Braves 1954-1965
Atlanta Braves 1966-1974
Milwaukee Brewers 1975-1976
Hall of Fame 1982

GAMES *(3rd all time)*	**3,298**
AT BATS *(2nd all time)*	**12,364**
BATTING AVERAGE	
Career	**.305**
Season High	**.355**
BATTING TITLES	**1956, 1959**
SLUGGING AVERAGE	
Career	**.555**
Season High	**.669**
HITS	
Career *(3rd all time)*	**3,771**
Season High	**223**
DOUBLES	
Career *(8th all time)*	**624**
Season High	**46**
TRIPLES	
Career	**98**
Season High	**14**
HOME RUNS	
Career *(1st all time)*	**755**
Season High	**47**
TOTAL BASES *(1st all time)*	**6,856**
EXTRA BASE HITS *(1st all time)*	**1,477**
RUNS BATTED IN	
Career *(1st all time)*	**2,297**
Season High	**132**
RUNS	
Career *(2nd all time)*	**2,174**
Season High	**127**
WORLD SERIES	**1957, 1958**
MOST VALUABLE PLAYER	**1957**

Aaron outlasted generations of sluggers. He began his career with sluggers Eddie Mathews and Joe Adcock; at the age of 39, in 1973, he joined teammates Darrell Evans and Davey Johnson to form the only trio of sluggers on one team ever to hit 40 or more homers in the same season.

Aaron kept his commitment to the civil rights movement out of the headlines. The black star of major league baseball's first team in the deep South, Aaron answered the inevitable taunts with his performance at the plate. He aimed to please—and for the left field bleachers. "As a black man going into the South, I wanted to please the crowd," Aaron said. "Left field was an attractive target, so I stopped going to right field, but relied on my quick wrists to pull the ball. No, I didn't hit for average anymore, but. . . ."

As few players have before or since, Aaron got better as he got older. He stayed in superb physical condition and moved inexorably toward one of baseball's most cherished records. In 1971, at age 37, Aaron had his best year ever, hitting .327 with a career-high 47 homers. Still 75 homers behind Babe Ruth's 714, Aaron continued his remarkable chase, hitting 34 homers in 1972 and 40 in just 392 at-bats in 1973. Aaron's 10.2 home run percentage in 1973 was the best of his career, and he ended the season with 713 homers, one short of Ruth.

Aaron insisted he wasn't trying to replace Ruth as an American icon and tried to downplay the comparison. "If I hit 750 home runs, it would just be that I hit 750 home runs. That's all," he said. Besides, the two were completely different players and personalities. Aaron used bat speed and powerful wrists to hit line drive homers, while Ruth relied on prodigious shoulders and forearms for his towering fly ball homers. As a personality, Aaron was much closer to Lou Gehrig than Ruth.

But the comparison persisted, and the hate mail poured in. "I don't care if they boo," Aaron said. "They pay their money, and they're entitled to that. But they call me nigger and every other word you can imagine. I just won't take that."

Mathews, Aaron's manager in 1974, said that that season "had aspects of a nightmare. We had to change Hank's name, hide him in the hotels, hire special limousines to chauffeur him in. Hundreds of writers and TV cameramen dogged him in the clubhouse. It was a mess. Very few people could have handled it as well as Hank did."

Aaron wasted no time once the season started, tying Ruth's record with a homer off Cincinnati's Jack Billingham in his first at-bat in the season opener. Benched for the rest of the series, Aaron and the Braves returned home April 8 to challenge history and the Dodgers. A light drizzle fell as the pregame circus began. Aaron's life was dramatized on a huge color map of the United States painted across the outfield grass. A choir serenaded him and Pearl Bailey sang the national anthem as a national television audience watched. Georgia Governor Jimmy Carter, Atlanta Mayor Maynard Jackson, and Sammy Davis Jr. were there, but Commissioner of Baseball Bowie Kuhn was absent because of a "previous commitment." The usually impassive Aaron was justifiably indignant. "How many other opportunities will a commissioner have to see Babe Ruth's record broken?" Aaron asked. "If I were white, he'd be here."

More than 53,000 fans were there. Now all Aaron had to do was hit a homer.

Dodger starting pitcher Al Downing walked Aaron in the second inning. In the fourth, Aaron drove a 1–0 fastball over the left center field fence. Skyrockets arched through the rain and Braves' mascot Chief Noc-a-Homa put a little something extra into his dance of celebration. Aaron circled the bases slowly and was greeted at home by his father—Herbert Aaron, Sr.—who leaped from his field-level box seat and outran everybody to be first to welcome baseball's new home run king.

Atlanta relief pitcher Tom House had snatched Aaron's homer from a fan's waiting net and raced toward home with the entire bullpen crew in tow. With characteristic brevity, Aaron answered those who suggested he had purposely waited to come to Atlanta to break the record. "I have never gone out on a ballfield and given less than my level best," he said. "When I hit it tonight, all I thought about was that I wanted to touch all the bases."

In 1956 (below) Aaron won his first batting title and led the league in hits and doubles. By the time he broke Ruth's record with his 715th home run in 1974 (above), he was atop almost all hitting categories.

Power at the Plate

B*all—traveling 90 miles per hour—meets bat, and its path is violently reversed. The sound is still the most reliable attention-getter in sports. Heads follow the ball's flight, and seats empty. The outfielder glides back to the wall, then becomes just another spectator. The ball lands, souvenir hunters scramble, and the game stops to honor its favorite son, the slugger.*

Preceding page: Mickey Mantle, New York Yankees. Above, Dave Winfield, New York Yankees; at right, Jody Davis, Chicago Cubs.

Clockwise from top right: Rick Schu, Baltimore Orioles; David Green, St. Louis Cardinals; Bo Jackson, Kansas City Royals; Dwight Evans, Boston Red Sox.

Above, Willie Mays, San Francisco Giants; right, Willie McCovey, San Francisco Giants; far right, Cal Ripken Jr., Baltimore Orioles.

Clockwise from far right:
Harmon Killebrew,
Minnesota Twins; Gregg
Jefferies, New York Mets;
Andre Dawson, Chicago
Cubs.

*Clockwise from above; George Brett,
Kansas City Royals; Reggie Jackson,
California Angels; Pete O'Brien, Texas
Rangers.*

Hack Wilson had a simple approach to hitting. "I just go up there with the intention of knocking the ball out of the park and swing." The approach worked, as Wilson won or shared the NL home run title four times from 1926 through 1930.

The Casey Syndrome

Somewhere men are laughing,
Somewhere children shout.
But there is no joy in Mudville.
Mighty Casey has struck out!

n 1908, winding up one of the great pennant races of all time, the Tigers, White Sox, and Indians raced toward the finish. The Indians were driven by their popular manager, arguably the finest second baseman of all time, Napoleon Lajoie. On October 3rd, the Sox and Indians dueled before the largest crowd in Cleveland history. The day before, the Indians' Addie Joss had pitched a perfect game, beating spitball specialist Ed Walsh, 1–0.

Chicago took a 3–2 lead into the seventh, when outfielder Patsy Dougherty muffed an easy fly for a two-base error. After a strikeout, an infield error, a steal, and another walk loaded the bases in the bottom of the seventh, the Naps—the nickname Lajoie's fans used for the hometown heroes—were ready to turn the game around.

In desperation, Chicago brought back Ed Walsh to quell the flare-up. The first man to face him was Bill Hinchman, hitting only .231, but "a tough man in a pinch." He fell for a Walsh spitball on the inside and slapped it to short for a force-out at home. That brought up the great Lajoie with two out and the bases still loaded.

Napoleon stared down his adversary. He had punched out two doubles that day but had uncharacteristically bobbled a throw by catcher Harry Bemis

Third strikes—especially called ones—give umpires a chance to inject a shot of theatrics into the game.

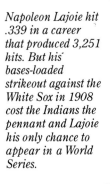

Napoleon Lajoie hit .339 in a career that produced 3,251 hits. But his bases-loaded strikeout against the White Sox in 1908 cost the Indians the pennant and Lajoie his only chance to appear in a World Series.

to set up two of the three Chicago runs. If ever retribution was overdue, this was the time, and Lajoie knew it. So did more than 20,000 Clevelanders.

"His weakness was a fastball, high and right through the middle," Walsh said. "If you pitched inside to him, he'd tear a hand off the third baseman. If you pitched outside, he'd knock the second baseman down. I tried him with a spitball that broke to the inside and down. Lajoie hit it so hard, it curved 20 feet before it passed third base. Foul, strike one. My next pitch was a spitter on the outside." Lajoie fouled it back into the stands.

Catcher Billy Sullivan called for another spitter, but Walsh just stared at him. Another sign. Another stare. Still a third one. Sully trotted to the box. "What's the matter?" he asked.

"I'll give him a fast one," Walsh said. Sully was dubious but finally agreed. It was an overhand, rising fastball, and Lajoie watched it go by in disbelief. "Strike three!" roared umpire Silk O'Loughlin. From the stands, shocked silence. "Lajoie sort of grinned toward me and tossed his bat toward the bench without ever a word."

Ed Walsh lived to be 78 years old. He always said the highlight of his career was whiffing Napoleon Lajoie with the bases loaded. "Not many pitchers ever did that."

If a game-winning home run is the slugger's glory, striking out in the clutch is the ultimate disgrace. For many who call themselves sluggers, striking out is the price that must be paid in going for the home run. The toughest of longball hitters do it. Mickey Mantle, Duke Snider, and Boog Powell are just three of the many who have done it twice in a single inning. The likes of Gorman Thomas and Dave Kingman have gone down swinging

five times in a game. But the best of the breed will humble pitchers for every strikeout they deliver.

The slugger who drove the hardest bargain with pitchers is Joe Di-Maggio. In 13 years of major league slugging, Joltin' Joe clipped 361 homers yet chalked up only 369 strikeouts. That works out to about one per homer. That's also one reason the Yankee Clipper put together the longest hitting streak ever: he generally hit the ball somewhere. In his streak year, 1941, DiMaggio hit 30 homers and fanned only 13 times— belting 2.3 home runs for each strikeout. In 1950 Ted Williams came close to duplicating DiMaggio's remarkable feat, hitting 28 homers and going down on strikes just 21 times.

By comparison, Willie Stargell paid 1,936 strikeouts for his 475 homers. Reggie Jackson slugged 563 homers and struck out a record 2,597 times doing it. In one September game in 1968, he too did it five times.

"I was never depressed after striking out," Hall of Fame member Stargell writes. "I was a confident hitter at the plate. I wasn't afraid to take a chance." And if he struck out a lot? "I saw that as a good sign. The more chances I took the more times I succeeded. I led the league in the ratio of chances taken. I was proud of that fact."

Stargell's opinions are shared by Jackson. "Striking out is no worse than grounding out or popping out. Baseball pays off on homers, not strikeouts."

While that kind of self-confidence is a decided plus—and in sharp contrast to DiMaggio's notorious modesty—the facts just don't bear Stargell and Jackson out. Statistically, the strikeout is unquestionably the worst out a hitter can make short of hitting into a double play. A ground ball may advance a runner or be booted for an error. A fly ball may be misjudged or score a runner from third. But the only good thing that can happen on a strikeout is for the

Even more impressive than his power, speed and grace was Joe DiMaggio's consistency as a hitter. No slugger in baseball history was tougher to strike out than "Joltin' Joe."

The New Caseys

In 1968, Mickey Mantle's career total 1710 strikeouts was a major league record. Twenty years later, Mantle's total ranks only eighth on the all-time strikeout list.

Career Leaders Through 1968

Player	Strikeouts
1. **Mickey Mantle**	**1710**
2. **Eddie Mathews**	**1487**
3. Babe Ruth	1330
4. Jimmie Foxx	1311
5. Duke Snider	1237
6. **Harmon Killebrew**	**1154**
7. **Willie Mays**	**1147**
8. Gil Hodges	1137
9. Ernie Banks	1088
10. Joe Adcock	1059
11. **Frank Robinson**	**1047**
12. **Frank Howard**	**1027**
13. Larry Doby	1011
14. Ken Boyer	1010
15. Hank Aaron	991
16. Roberto Clemente	997
17. Bob Allison	974
18. Dolf Camilli	961
19. Dick Stuart	936
20. Woodie Held	925

Career Leaders Through 1988

Player	Strikeouts
1. Reggie Jackson	2597
2. Willie Stargell	1936
3. Tony Perez	1867
4. Mike Schmidt	1866
5. Dave Kingman	1816
6. Bobby Bonds	1757
7. Lou Brock	1730
8. **Mickey Mantle**	**1710**
9. **Harmon Killebrew**	**1699**
10. Lee May	1570
11. Dick Allen	1556
12. Willie McCovey	1550
13. **Frank Robinson**	**1532**
14. **Willie Mays**	**1526**
15. Rick Monday	1513
16. Greg Luzinski	1495
17. **Eddie Mathews**	**1487**
18. **Frank Howard**	**1460**
19. Jimmy Wynn	1427
20. George Foster	1419

Boldface indicates player's appearance on both lists.

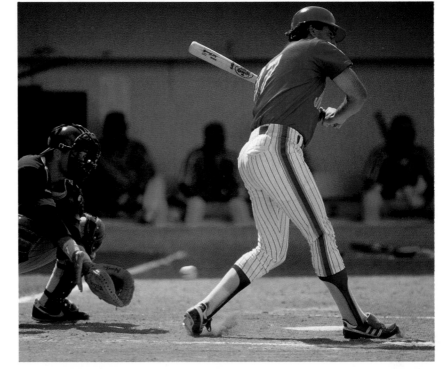

New York Mets first baseman Keith Hernandez has paid his price for home runs—the more homers he hit, the more often he struck out.

catcher to drop the third strike, which almost never happens. A strikeout, then, does nothing.

Did Willie and Reggie pay too high a price for their home runs? They certainly hit a lot of them, but they also gave pitchers a lot of crucial outs. Actually, their teams paid the price and probably figured it was worth it. Jackson and Stargell themselves were paid handsomely for their homers, and strikeouts don't loom large in sluggers' salary negotiations.

When Ted Williams took over as manager of the Washington Senators in 1969, he helped Frank Howard cut his strikeouts by a third, double his walks, add 22 points to his batting average, and hit 48 home runs, four more than in the previous year. If Williams had had a chance to manage Jackson and Stargell, one wonders what miracles he might have wrought.

There's no question that the tendency of today's sluggers to go for broke and damn the strikeouts pays off in fan appeal and adds a sense of drama and glory to the game. And when a wounded Kirk Gibson homers in the winning run in the bottom of the ninth, as he did in the first game of the 1988 World Series, it's the kind of heroism that would make Casey cringe.

It wasn't always so. In the post–World War II power era there was still a sense of balance in going for the long ball while keeping unnecessary outs to a minimum.

As a rookie in 1946, the Pirates' Ralph Kiner led the league in home runs with 23 and in strikeouts with a whopping 109. Reflecting on his free-swinging achievement, he admits "a lot of it was inexperience." Hank Greenberg moved to Pittsburgh the next year and roomed with Kiner, drilling him on the impor-

Reggie Jackson, with the Yankees, Athletics, Orioles, and Angels, became baseball's king of swing—and miss.

A modest man, Ernest Thayer (shown above with his wife) in 1888 created the most unbridled of baseball's literary characters. A century later, American sculptor Mark Lundeen chose Casey's image to fashion in bronze because of his own baseball experience as a youth.

Willliam DeWolf Hopper, actor

Casey at the Bat

On June 3, 1888, the San Francisco *Examiner* published the verses that have become one of America's best-loved poems. The piece was bylined "Phinn," and while there have been other claimants, it is generally accepted that it was written by Ernest Lawrence Thayer. Massachusetts born, Harvard educated, and a confirmed baseball crank, Thayer at 25 had been contributing humorous ballads for the paper's Sunday supplement, on assignment from none other than William Randolph Hearst, a former classmate who knew Thayer's work from the *Harvard Lampoon.* Thayer got his usual fee — $5.

In the late 1880s the National League had been playing a decade, stars like Mike "King" Kelly and Cap Anson were household words, and baseball fever raged throughout the country. The poem was well received but soon forgotten . . . almost. In New York City that autumn, the Giants hosted a theatrical performance for the visiting Chicago White Stockings and the evening cried out for something special for the big league heroes. The call went to a young performer named William DeWolf Hopper, and he rose to the occasion with a histrionic rendition of *Casey* that brought the house down.

Recognizing a good thing when he heard it, Hopper continued to declaim the poem from stages all over the country and became famous doing it — a good 10,000 times, by his own count.

The poem itself, which has been dismissed by some as simply charming doggerel, has become an American classic. It has been published widely, set to music, recorded, and parodied. It has even been made into silent films and a Disney cartoon, and in the 1950s it inspired an opera.

As far as Hopper was concerned, and virtually all America for that matter, *Casey at the Bat* was just an anonymous piece of verse. It was not until Hopper delivered his by now classic oration one evening in Worcester, Massachusetts, that he was unexpectedly introduced to the poet himself. The two couldn't have been less alike: Hopper the flamboyant vaudevillian; Thayer a quiet, unassuming businessman, content to let his authorship of the poem be forgotten. His rendition of the work, according to Hopper, was "the worst he had ever heard," and Thayer, who lived well into his seventies, steadfastly refused to accept a penny in royalty for the thousands of times his gem was reprinted.

And who was the real Casey? Dozens of ballplayers, amateur and professional, have been nominated over the years as the model for our folkloric antihero, none of them convincingly. According to Thayer in a 1938 letter to the Syracuse *Post-Standard,* the inspiration really came from

> . . . my enthusiasm for college baseball, not as a player, but as a fan. The poem has no basis in fact. The only Casey was not a ballplayer. He was a big, dour Irish lad of my high school days. I ventured to gag, as we say, this Casey boy. He didn't like it and he told me so, and, as he discoursed his big, clenched, red hands were white at the knuckles. I suspect the incident, many years after, suggested the title for the poem. God grant he never catches me."

A Ballad of the Republic Sung in the Year 1888

The outlook wasn't brilliant for the Mudville nine that day:
The score stood four to two with but one inning more to play.
And then when Cooney died at first, and Barrows did the same,
A sickly silence fell upon the patrons of the game.

A straggling few got up to go in deep despair. The rest
Clung to that hope which springs eternal in the human breast;
They thought if only Casey could but get a whack at that—
We'd put up even money now with Casey at the bat.

But Flynn preceded Casey, as did also Jimmy Blake,
And the former was a lulu and the latter was a cake;
So upon that stricken multitude grim melancholy sat,
For there seemed but little chance of Casey's getting to the bat.

But Flynn let drive a single, to the wonderment of all,
And Blake, the much despis-ed, tore the cover off the ball;
And when the dust had lifted, and the men saw what had occurred,
There was Johnnie safe at second and Flynn a-hugging third.

Then from 5,000 throats and more there rose a lusty yell;
It rumbled through the valley, it rattled in the dell;
It knocked upon the mountain and recoiled upon the flat.
For Casey, mighty Casey, was advancing to the bat.

There was ease in Casey's manner as he stepped into his place;
There was pride in Casey's bearing and a smile on Casey's face.
And when, responding to the cheers, he lightly doffed his hat,
No stranger in the crowd could doubt 'twas Casey at the bat.

Ten thousand eyes were on him as he rubbed his hands with dirt;
Five thousand tongues applauded when he wiped them on his shirt.
Then while the writhing pitcher ground the ball into his hip,
Defiance gleamed in Casey's eye, a sneer curled Casey's lip.

And now the leather-covered sphere came hurtling through the air,
And Casey stood a-watching it in haughty grandeur there.
Close by the sturdy batsman the ball unheeded sped—
"That ain't my style," said Casey. "Strike one," the umpire said.

From the benches, black with people, there went up a muffled roar,
Like the beating of the storm-waves on a stern and distant shore.
"Kill him! Kill the umpire!" shouted someone on the stand;
And it's likely they'd have killed him had not Casey raised his hand.

With a smile of Christian charity great Casey's visage shone;
He stilled the rising tumult; he bade the game go on;
He signaled to the pitcher, and once more the spheroid flew;
But Casey still ignored it, and the umpire said, "Strike two."

"Fraud!" cried the maddened thousands, and echo answered fraud;
But one scornful look from Casey and audience was awed.
They saw his face grow stern and cold, they saw his muscles strain,
And they knew that Casey wouldn't let that ball go by again.

The sneer is gone from Casey's lip, his teeth are clenched in hate;
He pounds with cruel violence his bat upon the plate.
And now the pitcher holds the ball, and now he lets it go,
And now the air is shattered by the force of Casey's blow.

Oh, somewhere in this favored land the sun is shining bright;
The band is playing somewhere, and somewhere hearts are light,
And somewhere men are laughing, and somewhere children shout;
But there is no joy in Mudville—mighty Casey has struck out.

tance of waiting for a good pitch to hit, of not swinging at pitches until he had to. Kiner cut his strikeouts by 28 and increased his homers by precisely the same number. The fact that Kiner was the NL home run king for seven years straight proves he learned something.

"We weren't trying to hit home runs every time," says former New York Giants first baseman Johnny Mize, who tied Kiner for NL home run honors with 51 in 1947, striking out only 42 times in the process. "When you're down to two strikes, you're trying to hit the ball some place, to guard the dish. Now these guys swing just as hard at the 0–2 as on the first pitch."

Unlike Williams, Big John was not finicky about waiting for perfect pitches. "If there's a man on third and one out, I didn't mind going outside and reaching for a ball that I could hit to the opposite field. I hated to leave that man on third base." Giant manager Mel Ott used to pay $2 for bringing a man in from third; it was a dollar fine for stranding him there. "I got quite a few bucks out of him," Mize says.

Yogi Berra really had a reputation as a bad-ball hitter, yet he was as stingy with strikeouts as anyone—only 1.2 whiffs per homer. Playing most of his career with such a huge strike zone, how could Yogi have struck out so seldom? "I honestly can't tell you," he shrugs. "I just saw the ball and I hit it." In one of his rare strikeouts, he swung at a pitch over his head, missed it, and stomped back to the dugout muttering "That ___ is so wild, I don't see how he can stay in the majors!"

Even Babe Ruth, who held the strikeout record in his day—long since smashed—was way ahead of the pitchers with a very respectable strikeout-to-home-run ratio—less than two to one, about the same as patient, hard-hitting Hank Aaron.

Cubs right fielder Andre Dawson (opposite) rarely gets cheated at the plate. In 1987 he homered more often than he walked, 49–32.

Even as player-manager of the Cleveland Indians, Frank Robinson could not escape the futility of protesting a third strike.

The secret of pitching, Casey Stengel once explained, is to get the ball as close to the plate and as far from the bat as possible. When a power hitter is glaring down your throat exactly 60'6" away, with runners straining on the bases, 60,000 people yelling, and the ball game on the line, it takes a man of iron courage—or iron brains—to throw the ball anywhere near where the hitter can get his bat on it. That fact, which might be called the Pitcher Fear Factor, gives the hurler no real choice. The batter walks.

As Allie Reynolds said of pitching to Ted Williams, "I'm overmatched. If the game is close, I've got to walk him."

These two men, Ruth and Williams, were walked more than any other batters in history. Ruth has a slight lead—2,056 to 2,019—but Williams would be far out in front if he had played those five years he served in World War II and Korea.

The Babe figured that, since he'd never see a good pitch, he might as well swing at the best one he did see. Ted never would. How many more home runs would each have hit if he had gotten good balls to hit?

At that, both men were lucky. They had men waiting to hit in the on-deck circle who were almost as dangerous as they were—Lou Gehrig behind the Babe, and Jimmie Foxx, Bobby Doerr, Vern Stephens and others behind Williams. Without that factor working for them, their total walks might well exceed their hits.

People who thrive on baseball statistics have figured out that, on average, every home run puts 1.4 runs on the scoreboard and every walk adds up to a third of a run. If that's the case, pitchers are slightly ahead of the game if they walk a man four times for every homer they yield. Williams averaged almost four walks per homer, indicating that Ted and the pitchers had just about

The trick when getting called out on strikes is to appear as if you're the victim of some terrible injustice. Switch-hitting outfielder Reggie Smith did it from both sides of the plate and in both leagues.

For being one of the most aggressive hitters ever to play the game, Giants center fielder Willie Mays didn't strike out much—just once every seven at-bats and just 2.3 times for every home run.

broken even. Ruth, surprisingly, averaged just under three walks per homer, which means that the pitchers could have walked him much more often before they reached the break-even point.

"I can be a weapon *because* they won't pitch to me," Mike Schmidt once remarked. "I'm going to give you a chance to walk me. I'm going to beat you on a base on balls until you *prove* that you can put the ball in the strike zone. And then I'm going to whale it. . . . I got to get them to know they got to throw me fastballs in the strike zone." Actually, Schmidt drew less than three walks per homer, about average today. Pitchers would have been smart to walk him more . . . and Schmidt was just smart enough not to let them.

The strategic value of walking a big hitter is one of baseball's classic disputes. Depending on the situation, it can be argued that it is good pitching strategy to walk the strong hitter to get to a weaker slot in the lineup, or to set up potential inning-ending double plays. The risks, of course, are that walks make base runners, and base runners can keep rounding bases. The intentional walk often gets driven home by the next slugger in the lineup. Still, more batters might do as Ruth did and swing at the best ball they can find before they get a free pass. The odds are in their favor. ◖

MANTLE BLASTS
565 FT. HOME RUN

Mickey Mantle

t's a long drive from Spavinaw, Oklahoma, to Cooperstown, New York, and Mickey Mantle hit just about every pothole along the way. Blessed with great speed—he was timed at 3.1 seconds from home plate to first base—he was cursed by a series of leg injuries. A bruise from a high school football game developed into a lifelong bone disease. In 1951, a freak fall over a drain pipe in Yankee Stadium tore cartilage in Mantle's knee, putting him out of the World Series and into a hospital bed. One day later his father—the driving force in Mantle's development as a player—joined him in the hospital and died the following summer at the age of 40.

Mickey Mantle arrived in New York City the most ballyhooed rookie the game had ever seen and had to step into the epic shadow of Joe DiMaggio—his predecessor in center field and one of the most popular Yankees ever. Too many strikeouts stopped him before he got started, and he was sent to the minors midway through his rookie season.

Mantle's 18-year career was marked by injury, financial woes, and the ravages of a rowdy lifestyle. Mantle hired as his agent the first person who made him an offer and wound up facing a $250,000 breach-of-contract suit. He fell into a pattern of late nights and too much drinking with teammate buddies Whitey Ford and Billy Martin—thinking that he was destined for the same fate as his father and uncles, all of whom died young from Hodgkin's disease—which probably cut his career short by several years.

His troubles continued even after he retired, when he was banned from any association with baseball because he accepted a promotional job with a gambling casino.

But in his prime he had no peer on the playing field. In the 1950s and early 1960s, Mantle was quite simply the best player on the best team in baseball. He was named Most Valuable Player three times and played in 20 All-Star Games. He had ten .300-plus seasons and led the American League in runs scored six seasons. He led the league in walks five times and won four home run titles and three slugging average titles. In 1956 Mantle won the Triple Crown with one of the most productive offensive seasons in history—a .353 average, 52 home runs, and 130 RBI. Mantle also led the league in runs scored and slugging average that year.

Mantle ranks eighth on the all-time home run list with 536, and only he, Babe Ruth, Ralph Kiner, and Willie Mays have topped the single-season 50-homer mark more than once in their careers. Mantle used a powerful upper body and a quick bat to hit some of baseball's longest home runs—including one that came closer than anyone else's to clearing the right field roof in Yankee Stadium. For sheer home run distance, Mantle and Ruth stand alone, except that Mantle—thanks to his father—launched his rockets from both sides of the plate.

Mantle's father, Mutt, worked six days a week in the lead and zinc mines of northeast Oklahoma, but on Sundays he played baseball. An outstanding player who gave up a possible pro career in order to support his family, Mutt saw baseball as Mickey's way out of the mines and even named him after a baseball player—Hall of Fame catcher Mickey Cochrane of the Philadelphia Athletics. Mutt anticipated the introduction of platooning—playing right-handed batters only against left-handed pitchers, and vice versa—and started Mickey switch hitting at the age of 5.

MICKEY MANTLE

Outfield, First Base
New York Yankees 1951-1968
Hall of Fame 1974

GAMES	2,401
AT BATS	8,102
BATTING AVERAGE	
Career	.298
Season High	.365
BATTING TITLES	1956
SLUGGING AVERAGE	
Career	.557
Season High	.705
HITS	
Career	2,415
Season High	188
DOUBLES	
Career	344
Season High	37
TRIPLES	
Career	72
Season High	12
HOME RUNS	
Career *(8th all time)*	536
Season High *(7th all time)*	54
TOTAL BASES	4,511
EXTRA BASE HITS	952
RUNS BATTED IN	
Career	1,509
Season High	130
RUNS	
Career	1,677
Season High	132
WORLD SERIES	1951-1953
	1955-1958, 1960-1964
MOST VALUABLE PLAYER	
	1956, 1957, 1962

Yankee Stadium's vast center field was a showcase for Mantle's athletic ability. This catch robbed Chicago's Larry Doby on June 24, 1957. Yankee right fielder Hank Bauer (9) had the best view.

Mantle played with pain and excelled in spite of it. "I see him swing sometimes," said Boston's Carl Yastrzemski, "and even from the outfield you can see his leg buckle under him, and when he winces in pain, I wince too. That's the way ballplayers feel about Mantle."

Mantle was a splendid athlete and flourished under his father's tutelage. Yankee scout Tom Greenwade, who signed the 17-year-old Mantle right out of high school in 1949, said to Mutt, "I'll tell you this. You know more baseball than the father of any boy I ever signed." Mantle signed for $140 per month and a $1,100 bonus, figures determined by Mutt's demand that Mickey earn as much playing baseball as he would have working in the mines.

After a 1950 season in which he battered Class C pitching for 136 RBI and a .383 average, Mantle was invited to spring training and promptly set jaws dropping with his awesome power. In a game against the University of Southern California, Mantle hit home runs of more than 500 feet from each side of the plate. USC coach Rod Dedeaux said Mantle's left-handed shot "was like a golf ball going into orbit. It was hit so far it was like it wasn't real."

The regular season was a different story. On July 13, Yankee manager Casey Stengel sent Mantle down to Class AAA Kansas City. The slump continued—he went 0 for his next 22 at-bats—and he called his father and told him he wanted out of baseball. Mutt came to Kansas City and laid it on the line to his son: "If that's the way you're going to take this, you don't belong in baseball anyway. If you have no more guts than that, just forget about the game completely. Come back and work in the mines like me."

Mantle proceeded to tear up Class AAA pitching and was back with the Yankees in late August. He was their starting right fielder and leadoff hitter in the World Series against the crosstown Giants, and he started on the road to becoming the most prolific run producer in Series history. He played in 12 fall classics—the Yankees won seven of them — and holds all-time firsts with 18 home runs, 40 RBI, 42 runs scored, and 43 walks.

Mantle piled up World Series heroics to go along with his numbers. In 1952, his eighth-inning homer in Game 6 gave New York a 3–2 win over

Mantle attacked pitches with a solid weight shift, powerful hip rotation, and simply vicious swing.

Brooklyn to tie the Series, and in Game 7 his homer off 28-year-old rookie sensation Joe Black broke a sixth-inning 2–2 tie and lifted the Yankees to a 4–2 win. In 1953, Mantle's homer helped give the Yankees a 2–0 Series lead over Brooklyn. Then, after the Dodgers won games 3 and 4, he keyed an 11–7 Yankee win with a grand slam in Game 5. The Yankees went on to win a record-setting fifth straight world championship. Earlier that season, Mantle's power introduced the tape measure home run into baseball's lexicon. A Mantle blast out of Washington's Griffith Stadium inspired Yankees publicity director Red Patterson to pace off the homer at 565 feet.

Mantle exploded in 1955 for 37 homers and a .611 slugging average, and from 1955 to 1962 he averaged 40 homers, 101 RBI, and hit .315. New York won seven pennants and four World Series in that eight-year span.

In 1961, Roger Maris grabbed headlines by hitting 61 homers to break Babe Ruth's single-season record of 60, while the Yankees rolled up 109 wins. But Mantle wound up with a career-high 54 homers and actually had a higher home run percentage than Maris—10.5 to 10.3.

Mantle had his last great season in 1964, with 35 homers, 111 RBI, and a .303 batting average. He hit three World Series homers—one in the bottom of the ninth to win Game 3—scored eight runs, and drove in eight in the Yankees' seven-game loss to St. Louis.

Called a "$100,000 invalid" by *Newsweek* in 1966, Mantle's legs finally gave out during spring training in 1969, and he called it quits. His press conference was typically brief. "I'm not going to play any more baseball," he said.

Beneath a clear Arizona sky, Cubs outfielder Chico Walker prepares to step into a spring training batting cage. In his hand and in the foreground are the tools of his trade.

Lumber

J.A. "Bud" Hillerich, shown standing at right in the doorway, started as an apprentice in his father's Louisville, Kentucky, woodworking shop. This photograph was taken just a few years after Hillerich created a handmade bat for Louisville Eclipses star Pete Browning, a bat that began a long line of Louisville Sluggers.

Caps and uniform styles haven't been the only changes in a century. This baseball hero—who appeared on the inside of a cigar box in 1885—uses a heavy bat and a hands-apart grip favored by many early hitters.

They called him "the Old Gladiator." Pete Browning, star outfielder of the Louisville Eclipses, earned his nickname by wielding his powerful bat like a sword, slashing hits seemingly at will. Yet on this sunny spring afternoon in 1884, the stalwart Browning was trying to battle his way out of a deepening slump. To no avail. The Old Gladiator went hitless in front of the hometown crowd and, to make matters worse, broke his favorite bat on a high, inside fastball.

One of the fans cheering on Browning and his teammates that day was John Andrew "Bud" Hillerich, an 18-year-old apprentice woodworker. Lured by near-perfect weather and the chance to root for the Eclipses, Hillerich had sneaked out of his father's woodturning shop and hightailed it over to the ball park. After Browning splintered his prized bat, Hillerich overheard the slugger bemoaning his loss. Impulsively, he offered to make a replacement. The Old Gladiator accepted—in those early days only a few woodturners made baseball bats—and the two went to Hillerich's shop after the game.

Hillerich had never made a baseball bat before, but he had turned out thousands of bedposts, tenpins and balusters on his simple wood-turning lathe. The pair picked out a piece of sturdy white ash and young Bud went to work, painstakingly fashioning the new bat according to Browning's directions. Every few minutes Hillerich removed the bat from the lathe and passed it to Browning for several test swings. "Too heavy," the slugger would report, and the bat would undergo more spins under the chisel. They worked into the night, until Browning took a practice swing, smiled broadly, and pronounced his 37-inch, 46-ounce new bat "just right!"

The next day the Old Gladiator stepped up to the plate with Bud Hillerich's piece of handcrafted white ash and promptly slapped out a booming line

By the beginning of the 20th century, the J.F. Hillerich & Son company had gone from making bed posts and bowling pins to become the world's first baseball bat factory. In 1905, the signature of Pittsburgh Pirates second baseman Honus Wagner was the first ever to adorn the company's stock in trade, the Louisville Slugger.

drive. Then another. And another. Browning went three for three that day, pulled out of his slump, and went on to rack up a .402 batting average in 1887 and a career .343, one of the ten best ever. Impressed by the new bat, his teammates beat a path to the small Hillerich shop on Louisville's First Street and other big leaguers followed. The custom-made baseball bat, dubbed the "Louisville Slugger" after Browning, gave birth to an industry.

While many modern-day fans recognize the name Hillerich & Bradsby and its famous "Louisville Slugger," few realize that today's baseball bat is a far cry from the models used by Browning and his predecessors. The bat has undergone a remarkable evolution from the sticks and flat-sided clubs swung by the game's earliest players to the streamlined piece of precision-crafted northern Pennsylvania white ash favored by today's sluggers. Yet, while the bat's weight, dimensions and appearance may have changed over the last 150 years, players have consistently treated the tools of their trade with a combination of awe, respect, superstition and, at times, downright adoration. Pete Rose carried his to the ballpark in a customized leather tote, Richie Ashburn slept with his, and Frank Frisch hung his bats in a barn to "cure" like sausages during the off season. Former Boston slugger George Scott spoke for many hitters when he said, "If you wanna rumble, just touch my lumber."

In the early years of this century, many bats were labelled with colorful decals featuring premier players of the day. Jake Daubert won batting titles in 1913 and 1914 for the Brooklyn Dodgers.

The first bats were just straight sticks, and early players made their own from tool handles, wagon tongues, or other pieces of wood trimmed to size. When Hillerich introduced the custom-made bat in 1884, the heavy bat was in vogue since most hitters needed lots of mass to slap line drives with the dead ball. "Swinging for the fences" was unheard of, as players merely hoped to get on the basepaths. A savvy batter's success depended on

Ty Cobb used hundreds of different bats in his 24-year career, but the model that bore his nickname was the most popular with hitters through the 1920s.

A 1937 ad for other Louisville Sluggers (right) featured two dozen registered, autographed models. The Pepper Martin style (second from the bottom) could be had in saddle brown finish with the new "cone grip" knob at $24 a dozen.

A Harry H. Davis decal on your bat meant instant power. Davis was a true dead-ball slugger, winning four straight American League home run titles from 1904 to 1907 but never hitting more than twelve home runs in a season.

how well he could place the ball and keep it in play by driving it through holes in the infield or lofting it over the infielders' heads.

While the materials and methods for making bats have scarcely changed in a century, the shape, size and weight have evolved greatly, reflecting the way the game is played. There were no restrictions on bat size or shape until 1863, when the official rule book decreed that bats had to be round and no more than $2\frac{1}{2}$ inches in diameter at any one point. Sporting goods manufacturers began selling an assortment of "regulation" models. Peck and Snyder's 1875 catalog included bats made of willow, ash, spruce and basswood, featuring two models with flutes or ridges carved into their upper halves. Another was made from American willow and was loaded with a core of ash for extra strength. Most of these early models were long, from 36 to 40 inches, and had a very straight taper. They set a player back anywhere from 50 to 75 cents apiece. By today's standards, handles were thick, barrels thin, and the bats had little curvature. Pete Browning's first Louisville Slugger was over a yard long, weighed almost three pounds, and measured $1\frac{1}{2}$ inches at the handle with a straight taper to $2\frac{1}{2}$ at the barrel—a heavy, strong instrument.

A strange-looking four-sided bat made a brief appearance in the 1880s but was ruled ineligible for use in the major leagues. Proponents of this square bat claimed that "when a batsman becomes accustomed to the use of the new bat, sharp fly tips will be very rare from this bat, and foul balls will not be hit once in ten times as frequently as with the use of the round bat." Batters looked more like muggers than sluggers when they waved these fearsome slabs of lumber over home plate.

Major leaguers jumped on the flat bat bandwagon in 1885 when rules were amended to allow the use of the bunting bat, a bat that had been sawed

neatly in half lengthwise. All this flat bat business mercifully came to a halt in 1893 when the rule that the bat had to be round found its way back into the rulebooks, where it has remained to this day. In 1895 the legal diameter of the bat was increased to $2^3/_4$ inches.

A turn-of-the-century invention, the "mushroom" bat—so called because of its odd-shaped handle—found favor with some players. A 1904 advertisement for the Spalding Mushroom explained, "The knob arrangement at the end enables us to get a more even distribution of weight than is possible under the old construction." The ad also included a ringing endorsement for the mushroom bat from Tinkers, Evers, and Chance, the famed Chicago double-play trio. Players disenchanted with their mushrooms could opt for the "Pneumatico, the first real improvement in Base Ball Bats offered the player for years," as stated in a 1907 advertisement in *The Sporting News*. This ingenious bat boasted a hollowed-out core filled with rubber—a precursor of later, illegally doctored bats.

Shorter but not lighter bats came into favor after the turn of the century. Wee Willie Keeler, a turn-of-the-century advocate of the short bat, summed up his strategy in the famous advisory "hit 'em where they ain't!" Ty Cobb's favorite Louisville Slugger was typical of the times. It was $34^1/_2$ inches long, weighed 42 ounces, and had a smaller, more defined handle than Browning's. *Baseball Magazine* said in its August 1920 issue that "Ty has as many different bats as milady has hairpins, each to be used for a particular purpose. Cobb carries a special bat named after each pitcher of a rival club designed especially to correspond to the peculiarities of the particular moundsman." An exaggeration? Perhaps, but the Georgia Peach—who favored a hands-apart grip —did end up with a lifetime batting average of .367.

Before the invention of the bat rack, dugouts could be hazardous places, especially for catchers and infielders chasing pop fouls. The 1923 Yankees' dugout (above) was particularly dangerous for opposing pitchers as well. The Yankees got the most from their lumber that year, leading the American League with 105 home runs.

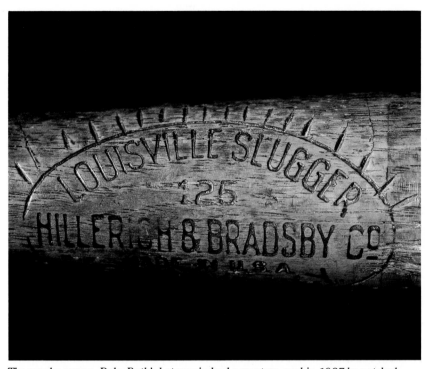

The way he swung, Babe Ruth's bat was indeed a weapon, and in 1927 he notched it—gunfighter style—for each home run he hit. But bats break, and this one, also shown on page 125, didn't last to number 60.

Detroit's Ty Cobb (opposite, right) brought an almost fanatical intensity to all aspects of his play—including the bats he selected. Cobb was a slashing, line-drive hitter and was famous for choking far up on the bat with his hands spread several inches apart.

Babe Ruth's love affair with the home run had a massive influence on both hitting styles and bat design in the 1930s. Frank "Wildfire" Schulte is credited with pioneering the curved taper design, but it was Babe Ruth who popularized it. Ruth's model was still quite heavy at 44 ounces, 35 inches long, with a medium-large handle and fat barrel. The profile of the Babe's bat is much more similar to Darryl Strawberry's than to Pete Browning's. Batters tried to emulate the Sultan of Swat and started hitting from their heels as they aimed for the fences. Lacking Ruth's power, they needed more bat speed for longball hitting and demanded lighter, longer bats. According to Hillerich & Bradsby vice president Rex Bradley, "Players wanted thinner handles and larger barrels so they could hold the bat in their fingers, not their palms, and get good 'whip' when the bat was swung." Bats suddenly took on a more contoured silhouette and looked much more like today's model than the bludgeonlike mallets used in Browning's era. Sluggers hit a lot more homers with their thinner, lighter bats. They also broke a lot more of them.

Bats continued to get lighter; by the 1950s they averaged 33 ounces, lighter by half a pound or more than at the turn of the century. Players explain that a lighter bat allows them to wait longer for a pitch and swing faster. And the results seem to bear them out. Hank Aaron broke Babe Ruth's career home run record with a Louisville Slugger that was ten ounces lighter than the Babe's. Roger Maris swore by his 32-ounce bat. Rex Bradley, a proponent of the lighter bat, observed, "No home-run hitter ever used a thick handled bat." Ted Williams agreed: "I see no percentage at all in using a heavy bat. You can get the same results by being quicker with a light bat." But let's leave the last word on light versus heavy to Joe Hauser, who played back in the 1920s. He swung a puny 32-ounce stick when most of his teammates favored

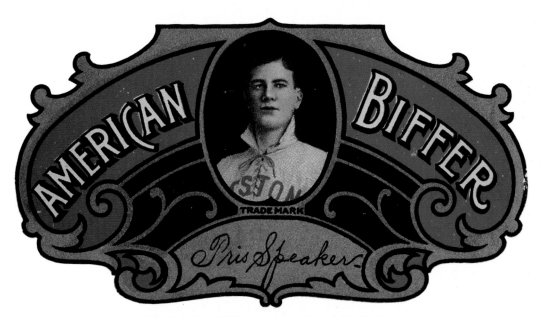

The American Biffer bat—manufactured by Stall and Dean in Brockton, Massachusetts and Chicago—featured superstars of its own, including Red Sox outfielder Tris Speaker, who hit 793 doubles in his 22-year career, more than anyone else.

37-ounce-and-up lumber. At the end of his career, Hauser smacked 69 homers in the minors one season and counseled his teammates, "You swing the wagon tongues and I'll stick to this buggy whip of mine!"

Thinner handles lightened bats, but hitters looked for even more ways of shaving off ounces. Stan Musial used to take a jackknife to his already thin handle and Jose Cardenal copied Japanese sluggers who used bats with hollowed-out barrels. The "teacup" style of bat was legalized in 1971, and bat makers added this Japanese-inspired design to their lines.

The bat of today, in keeping with a style of play that has even light-hitting Rick Dempsey swinging for the fences, has a very thin handle. It's relatively short—not more than 34 inches—and quite light, generally in the low to middle 30-ounce range. Because they are not as thick and sturdy as bats of yesteryear, broken bats are commonplace, and sluggers like Jim Rice have been known to snap bat handles on checked swings.

Since the 1960s the alluring whack of timber meeting horsehide has steadily been replaced by the much less alluring metallic ping of aluminum bats. Although they have not been approved for professional play, aluminum bats have taken over Little League, softball, and college ball. They don't break as easily as wooden bats, have larger sweet spots, and are easier to "whip." Studies have shown that balls hit with an aluminum bat travel faster than those hit with a wooden model. Indeed, they are so effective that many consider them too dangerous for the majors. As an Orioles coach, Frank Robinson once told the Baltimore *Sun,* "I don't think you'll ever see an aluminum bat in the majors because you could kill somebody hitting with those things."

All four major manufacturers—Hillerich & Bradsby, Rawlings (makers of Adirondack), Worth Sports Company, and Canada's Cooper—offer metal

Trimming the Bat

From the days of Pete Browning's very first Louisville Slugger, more and more batters have come to the plate wielding less and less.

Career Years	Player	Length inches	Weight ounces	Career Years	Player	Length inches	Weight ounces
1882-94	Pete Browning	37	44-48	1947-56	Al Rosen	36	36
1905-28	Ty Cobb	34 1/2	35-43	1947-61	Ted Kluszewski	35	35-39
1906-30	Eddie Collins	34	33-40	1951-68	Mickey Mantle	35	32-34
1912-27	Heinie Groh	34	39	1954-76	Hank Aaron	35-36	32-34
1913-29	Edd Roush	33	46-50	1956-76	Frank Robinson	36	35
1914-35	Babe Ruth	35-36	37-47	1961-83	Carl Yastrzemski	35	33
1915-37	Rogers Hornsby	34-35	37-39	1962-82	Willie Stargell	36 1/2	38
1923-39	Lou Gehrig	34	38	1963-86	Pete Rose	34-36	31-35
1924-44	Al Simmons	35-38	35-37	1967-87	Reggie Jackson	34 1/2	33
1936-51	Joe DiMaggio	36	34-35	1973-	George Brett	34 1/2	32
1939-60	Ted Williams	33-35	32-34	1976-	Dale Murphy	34 1/2	32
1941-63	Stan Musial	34 1/2	32-33	1982-	Wade Boggs	34 1/2	32
1946-59	Del Ennis	36	35-42	1982-	Tony Gwynn	32	30
1946-65	Yogi Berra	35	33	1985-	Jose Canseco	35	35

bats. In the early 1970s, Hillerich & Bradsby was turning out six million ash bats a year. Today, due to the rising popularity of the aluminum bat, the number of wooden bats in the market has dropped appreciably. And last year, Worth introduced its latest innovation—the graphite bat, which is every bit as effective as the aluminum bat and sounds right to boot. The Old Gladiator, not to mention Bud Hillerich, must be spinning in his grave.

Bats have evolved over the years, but the bond between a player and his bat has never changed. Ted Williams so treasured his bats that he traveled to Louisville before the start of every season and personally combed through Hillerich & Bradsby's lumberyard for the perfect piece of ash. To test the wood, he'd drop it on the factory's concrete floor and listen for just the right "plonk."

Once Williams returned a shipment of bats, complaining they were oversize. H&B employees checked the bats and discovered that the Boston outfielder was indeed correct—they were .005 inches too thick in the handle! He got his new bats. Intrigued by Williams' ability to gauge a bat's dimensions, Bud Hillerich once tested the legendary slugger. Williams remembers that Hillerich "put six bats on a bed, one at a time. One was a half-ounce heavier than the others. He had me close my eyes and pick the heavier bat. I picked it out twice in a row." Williams also dutifully cleaned his bats with alcohol every night and took them to the post office to weigh them until the Red Sox agreed to put a scale in the clubhouse.

Williams was by no means alone in his almost-mystical relationship with his bats. Bobby Murcer believed that the cold winds that blew through Candlestick Park could damage his bats. So he hid them away in the clubhouse sauna. Eddie Collins went Murcer one better. He buried his bats in a

Modern bats aren't complete without accessories. Atlanta's Dale Murphy wears two batting gloves and rubs a pine tar rag on the handle of his teacup bat for a better grip. The donut-shaped weight is handier for warming up than swinging two or three bats.

Tools of the Trade

This shorter, thicker bat was designed in the late 1880s for dead-ball hitters like Pop Anson. Like other players of this period, Anson experimented with different woods, including hickory covered with ash and split bamboo.

Spalding introduced its first line of trademarked bats in 1877, and in the 1890s offered a number of "black end bats" which ranged in price from 25 to 50 cents.

From 1892 to 1910, outfielder Wee Willie Keeler used the shortest bat ever in the major leagues—$30\frac{1}{2}$ inches. Keeler, who hit .432 in 1897, was one of the first players to have his name emblazoned on a Louisville Slugger.

In baseball's early days, most bats were long, straight and heavy. This 39-inch, 54-ounce trophy bat was turned from mahogany and given in 1874 to the Binghamton Iron Works team for their 27–23 win over the Cigar Makers.

Fungo bats—this one was used around 1900—are used to hit fly balls to fielders during pregame practice. The term dates back to 1867, and its likely derivation is the German word fangen, *meaning* to catch.

The early 1900s brought innovations like the "Ball Balanced" bat made by J.F. Hillerich & Son. The large knob provided a counterweight to the barrel, which supposedly provided a more balanced swing.

Boston sporting goods dealer Wright &
Ditson was one of many companies
that started turning bats in the early
1900s. Only a handful still make bats,
as 55—including Wright & Ditson—
have since gone out of business.

Third baseman Heine Groh, who played
from 1912 to 1927, designed the 34-inch,
39-ounce "bottle bat," which he used to
compile a .292 lifetime batting average.
Groh's design was a step toward today's
thinner handles and thicker barrels.

Ted Williams used this bat
in the 1957 All-Star Game.
He cleaned his bats with
alcohol and had a scale in
the Red Sox clubhouse to see
if his bats had picked up any
weight from dirt or
condensation.

The Pontiac Turning Company offered this tapered, almost knobless model in 1915. It was one of the many variations on the mushroom bat below.

Spalding came up with the "Mushroom Bat" in 1904, but others—including Piper—borrowed the design.

Aluminum bats were introduced in the late 1960s by companies like Alcoa and Reynolds Aluminum. Mizuno, a Japanese company, offers only aluminum bats in the United States, though Pete Rose got his last thousand hits with a Mizuno wood bat.

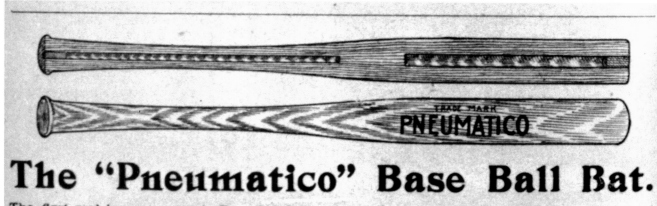

The "Pneumatico" Base Ball Bat.

The first real improvement in Base Ball Bats offered the player for years.   Proper weight and balance.   Most resilient and longest hitting bat on the market.

Electrotypes like above furnished for jobbers' catalogues on request.   Address

PNEUMATICO BAT CO., YORK, PA.

In 1907 the Pneumatico Bat Company offered sporting goods dealers yet another "improvement" on a basic design. The thick profile disguises a hollow core designed to enhance balance and power.

pile of horse manure "to keep them alive." Chicago Cubs manager Jim Frey used to soak his bats in motor oil and others anointed theirs with everything from linseed oil to corn oil to tobacco juice. Leon Durham goes beyond such mundane measures. He asks his mother to say a prayer over his bats before every game.

Johnny Pesky used to carry on a running conversation, albeit one-sided, with his bat. Minor league catcher Jim Kelly once drew a pair of eyes and glasses on his bat hoping to break out of an 0-for-16 slump. His newly decorated bat promptly rewarded him with two home runs. And in his record-setting season of 1927, Babe Ruth religiously notched his Louisville Slugger for the first 21 of his 60 home runs. Then his bat broke. Today the mended bat occupies pride of place in H&B's museum.

Tobacco juice, motor oil, and horse manure bat treatments may be outlandish but they are all legal. That's more than can be said for some of the methods baseball's cagier sluggers have used to "enhance," or doctor, their lumber. In the 1950s Ted Kluszewski hammered tenpenny nails into his bat to add weight, while others, such as Nellie Fox, illegally flattened their bats with a sledgehammer. Perhaps inspired by the Pneumatico, determined batters can be downright industrious when it came to bat doctoring. Stormin' Norman Cash knew how it was done. Cash's method was to drill out an eight-inch hole in the business end of his bat, stuff it with cork and sawdust, and top this with wood putty. Cash and other bat doctors were convinced their cork-filled bats delivered more bounce to the ball.

The award for Most Ingenious Substance Abuse in a Bat goes to Graig Nettles of the Yankees, who entertained fans and players alike in 1974 when he splintered his bat on a fly ball to right. Out from his doctored bat flew six

Today's major leaguers want light bats with thin handles to generate the bat speed and whip necessary to reach the bleachers. The down side is that such bats are not very sturdy, as Boston's Don Baylor (left) demonstrated.

high-pressure rubber "Super Balls." Out also was Dr. Nettles for contravening Rule 6.60d:

> Illegal bats: An illegal bat is one which has been tampered with in such a way that something unusual happens when the bat makes contact with the ball. The tampering usually involves filing, sanding, nailing, hollowing (and then filling with cork), grooving, flat surfacing, shaving and waxing. Any player caught using or trying to use an illegal bat may be thrown out of the game.

Former Baltimore Oriole manager Earl Weaver didn't hesitate to reveal that he swung a corked bat during his minor league days. "Back in 1955 when I was playing in New Orleans I hit six homers in the month of July with a cork-filled bat," wrote Weaver in his autobiography. "I never hit six homers in a season before or after that. Everyone on the team had a few of the corked bats and we went on a home run binge."

The question remains: Does the doctored bat really give batters an edge? Yes. And no. Peter Brancazio, a Brooklyn College physics professor, has brought both his scientific curiosity and a few computers to the question and has found that filling a bat with cork, rubber or whatever has virtually no effect. He told *Discover* magazine that "stuffing some foreign substance into a bat simply cannot make an average hitter a great hitter. Any benefit gained by using a hollowed-out bat could just as easily be obtained by using a lighter bat." H&B's Rex Bradley, who ought to know, agreed: "Using a corked bat is more mental than anything."

The typical ballplayer can go through dozens of bats a year. But as with other aspects of baseball, "typical" doesn't tell the whole story. Orlando

National League umpires John Kibler (right) and Charlie Williams play out a familiar 1987 scene—inspecting Howard Johnson's bat. The Mets third baseman hit 36 homers that year—three times his previous high—and his bats were confiscated and cut open several times, though no foreign matter was ever found.

Shoeless Joe Jackson swung one of the heaviest—and most productive—bats of the dead-ball era. He called it "Black Betsy." Author Bernard Malamud used it in his novel The Natural *as the inspiration for protagonist Roy Hobbes' magical bat "Wonderboy."*

Commercial bats are now made by machine, but the major league variety is still turned by hand. It takes a trained craftsman about ten minutes at the lathe to turn a piece of northern white ash into a professional bat.

Cepeda firmly believed that each bat had only one hit in it, and he'd toss out a bat when that quota was exhausted. Babe Ruth ordered more bats than any other player, not because he broke so many, but because he gave hundreds away as souvenirs. The stingiest batter of all time was Hall of Famer Joe Sewell, who swung only one bat in 7,132 major league trips to the plate between 1920 and 1933. Conversely, Texas Ranger outfielder Pete Incaviglia likes to take extra batting practice and regularly goes through more than 400 bats a year. (The team picks up the $7,000-plus annual tab.)

From the ax handle to the Louisville Slugger to the latest aircraft aluminum model, the baseball bat has held a special place in the hearts of every amateur and professional ballplayer. Perhaps the best description of this sometimes magical, sometimes mystical relationship is contained in Donald Gropman's biography of the legendary slugger "Shoeless Joe" Jackson. The Chicago player used his bat, "Black Betsy," to rack up a lifetime .356 average:

> She was 36 inches long and weighed about 48 ounces. But she was more than just a bat; she was Joe's talisman, his trademark, the handmark tool of his profession. She fit the grip of his hands so perfectly and sliced through the air so smoothly when he cut loose at the plate that it seemed as if some of the sweeping power came from her, seemed as if Black Betsy were alive and eager to whack the baseball as it came whistling to the plate.

Anyone who's ever relished that tantalizingly perfect moment when bat squarely meets ball knows that there's much more to a baseball bat than just 34 ounces of northern Pennsylvania white ash. ◑

This cracked and worn bat is one of the most venerable of them all. It was used by Babe Ruth in 1927 on the way to hitting 60 home runs (see page 115) and is now on exhibit at Slugger Park in Jeffersonville, Indiana, where Louisville Sluggers are now manufactured.

Going for the Fences

maine the NBA playing games in Boston with an eleven-foot basket and in Los Angeles with one at nine feet. The NFL playing in Chicago with a 110-yard field and in Washington with 90 yards—or in Dallas with goal posts on the goal line and in Miami ten yards behind it. Absurd. But that's the situation baseball has tolerated for more than a century. Early baseball fields were just that: open fields with the recognizable diamond and a lot of space all around it. As the game went professional in the late 1800s, provisions were made for spectators—simple rows of seats, sometimes with canopies to protect against sun and drizzle. Except for an absence of chain-link fence, they were not very different from the typical little league and softball fields thousands of kids play on today. But in those days, foul lines were infinite and outfields had no limit.

To accommodate paying spectators, grandstands were built, much like those common to race tracks and fairgrounds. Temporary bleachers could be assembled as needed, and grassy pastures could be roped off to accommodate overflow crowds or horse-drawn buggies, great grandfather's equivalent of today's sky boxes. Eventually, outfield fences appeared, cut and shaped to fit the vacant city lot they were built on, and the only spectators from that quarter were reckless boys lucky enough to find knotholes.

In older stadiums, the fences could be very short. In Lake Front Park, Chicago, the foul lines extended less than 200 feet from the plate, and balls hit over the fence were ground rule doubles. In 1884 the rules changed, opening up heroic possibilities: a ball over the fence in the air was an automatic home

For fans and sluggers who dislike the symmetry and uniformity of modern ballparks, Chicago's Wrigley Field is a treat. Ivy still covers its brick outfield walls, and the scoreboard has hardly changed since 1937.

New York's Polo Grounds, set in Coogan's Hollow, was always the most dramatic of ballparks. As far back as 1905 the left and right field bleachers were invitingly close, but center field stretched toward infinity.

run, and a banjo-hitting ex-pitcher, Ned Williamson, popped 27 homers for a record that stood until Babe Ruth hit 29 in 1919.

But mostly the old parks were mammoth, with some center fields receding 600 feet or more toward the horizon. As permanent bleachers were built, the distances shrank. And with the post-Ruthian emphasis on the long ball, owners found other ways to help a home-town slugger. One way was to put bullpens in the outfield. In 1940 the Red Sox constructed "Williamsburg," the bullpens in right field, just for Mr. Williams. They're still there in Fenway.

In 1947 the Pirates built "Greenberg Gardens," or "Kiner's Corner," in left, to help their two big guns. After Greenberg and Kiner left, so did the bullpen. The impish Bill Veeck confided that, in Cleveland, his groundskeepers moved the wire fence in or out a few feet overnight depending on which team was coming to town or who was scheduled to pitch. Veeck was also responsible for planting the ivy that covers the outfield walls in Wrigley Field. More than one hitter has taken an extra base on a ball that had to be rooted out of the ivy jungle, although today a ball lost in the ivy is a ground rule double.

Quirky ballparks disconcerted hitters and handicapped fielders throughout the first two-thirds of this century, and only in the last few decades have major league playing fields become reasonably uniform. Washington's old Griffith Stadium featured a high angular fence jutting into center like a wedge, separating the field from the adjacent apartment house. Ebbets Field had its famous sloping wall in right field, and Crosley Field featured an outfield that sloped upwards in deep left.

In the past, *where* you played could be more important than *how* you

47 FT.

Once outfield fences were installed
throughout the Polo Grounds, relief
pitchers' backs were always against the
wall. Warming up in fair territory was
even more disconcerting.

Boston's Fenway Park is baseball's most intimate arena. It holds the fewest fans—33,583—of any major league ballpark, but its narrow foul ground and irregular dimensions provide sightlines that make every play an adventure.

played. Mel Ott, kicking his foot up as he swung, could golf seven-iron shots into the right field upper deck overhang in the Polo Grounds barely 250 feet away. In contrast, Joe DiMaggio could whale a drive deep into Yankee Stadium's "Death Valley" almost 200 feet farther than Ott's drives—where Ted Williams would pull it down after a long, gangly gaited gallop.

The vast confines of Yankee Stadium, which was more a house built for Ruth than it was The House That Ruth Built, featured a 296-foot "short porch" in right as a target for the Babe. Although the great left-handed hitter didn't take full advantage of it, slugging a lot of 400-foot outs to deep center, it has nonetheless beckoned to other Yankee lefties over the years—among them Lou Gehrig, Bill Dickey, Charlie Keller, Tommy Henrich, Yogi Berra, Roger Maris, Bobby Murcer, Graig Nettles, and Don Mattingly.

For decades Yankee Stadium was only 301 feet down the left field line, a foot less than Fenway's right field foul pole. But in both parks the stands slanted away quickly to 400-feet plus. The Yankees always had their share of big right-handed hitters like Joe DiMaggio, Joe Gordon, Bill Skowron, Dave Winfield and Jack Clark, who had to cope with the vast acreage of Death Valley in left. To give the visiting Yankees some of their own medicine, Athletics owner Charley Finley once built his own temporary right field "short porch" in Kansas City, matching Yankee Stadium's right field dimensions. It caused a stir in exhibition games, but the league told him to tear it down for the regular season. He tore it down.

The oval Polo Grounds was only 258 feet to extreme right and 287 to left, but it also fell away rapidly to 483 in deep center, between the twin bleachers. Lou Brock hit only 149 homers, but one of them dropped into those center field bleachers, which not even Ruth ever reached. In fact, only two other men

Washington's Griffith Stadium—426 feet to left, 328 to right, and 421 to center—was tough on home run hitters, so Senators' teams weren't built around power. But they apparently weren't built around speed either, as the route from home plate to first base was graded downhill.

The Green Monster in Boston's Fenway Park can be a mixed blessing for sluggers. Kansas City's Bo Jackson watches as a fly ball clears the 37-foot-high left field wall, but many line drives that would be homers in other parks are played deftly off the wall, and sluggers are held to singles.

ever did—Hank Aaron and Joe Adcock. Of the three balls hit to the Polo Grounds' bleachers in more than 50 years of play, Brock and Adcock did it on successive days.

Shoeless Joe Jackson was the first man ever to clear the roof of the Polo Grounds, and only two other men duplicated the feat, neither of them in Giant uniforms. Babe Ruth, who said he patterned his swing after Jackson's, did it several times—once in a World Series, once in an exhibition game against Lefty Grove. The third was Rube Walker as a reserve catcher for the Dodgers in the 1951 playoff. It was his fourth and last homer of the year.

The Polo Grounds' short left field lower deck is where Bobby Thomson's home run won that legendary playoff, but in virtually any other stadium it would have been just another long line drive out. "It's the worst place I could have been traded," says John Mize, who still hit a lot of home runs for the Giants. Unlike Mel Ott, he didn't pull the ball and wasted a lot of long drives into deep right center. A generation earlier, Bill Terry had done the same thing. Ironically, Mize was traded away from St. Louis, where Sportsmen's Park was a chummy 310 feet away down the right field line. Stan Musial loved it!

By contrast, the left field fence in Ebbetts Field was some 60 feet deeper than the Polo Grounds—348 at the foul line. But the stands made an acute angle with the foul line so that in the power alley, the seats were actually a bit less than 348 feet away—duck soup for right-handed Dodger sluggers.

Cheapest homers of all were hit to right field in Philadelphia's Baker Bowl—"the Bandbox"—where a Fenway-type wall reared behind the first baseman some 30 feet closer than Boston's Green Monster. Chuck Klein became adept at lifting short high flies over it; when he was traded to Chicago, his home run totals abruptly plunged. The Phils' Cy Williams, who led the NL

Pittsburgh's Forbes Field offered many obstacles to sluggers. In left field alone there was a huge scoreboard and a fence around the light standard. Pirate second baseman Bill Mazeroski managed to miss them all with his game-winning homer in the bottom of the ninth in Game 7 of the 1960 World Series against the Yankees.

Yankee Stadium is still the site of three of baseball's most familiar landmarks—center field monuments to Babe Ruth, Lou Gehrig, and Miller Huggins. But after the stadium's outfield was reconfigured in 1976 and again in 1985, its dimensions became less daunting, and the monuments out of play.

in homers four times, and even the right-handed Gavvy Cravath regularly pumped fly balls over it.

Tenants of quirky stadiums like Fenway Park and Ebbets Field simply designed teams around their parks. The Red Sox especially loved powerful right handers—Jimmie Foxx, Rudy York, Vern Stephens, Walt Dropo, Dick Stuart, Tony Conigliaro, Jim Rice, Tony Armas. The Dodgers also loaded the lineups with right handers Gil Hodges, Roy Campanella, Carl Furillo, and Jackie Robinson. The result was that when either club visited Yankee Stadium it had the wrong kind of team on the field and paid the price.

In 1958, when the Dodgers moved from Brooklyn to the Los Angeles Coliseum—an oval stadium built for the 1932 Olympics—the right field power alley was 440 feet away, but left field was 250 feet at the foul pole. The Dodgers put up a screen to help somewhat, but Wally Moon became famous for lifting little "Moon shots" over it, even though Moon was left handed and far from a slugger. The Dodgers' big left-handed Duke Snider, meanwhile, had to change his hitting style to survive.

Willie Stargell played seven years in Pittsburgh's old Forbes Field, with its high screen in front of the right field stands. He estimates he lost 22 homers a year there. That's 154 home runs. Added to his 475 total, it would have given him more than 625 for a career. His estimate may not be far off. In his last year in Forbes, 1969, he hit 29. In his first full year in the new Three Rivers Stadium, 1971, he hit 48.

Walls vary in height as well as distance, from the belt-high wall in the old Yankee Stadium to the 30- to 50-foot Everests that loomed over some other parks. Fenway Park's Green Monster is an inviting target to right-handed hitters without much power, such as Bucky Dent. "But it has hurt me as much

Built in 1910, Chicago's Comiskey Park is baseball's oldest stadium. Only four players—Hank Greenberg, Alex Johnson, Dick Allen, and Richie Zisk—ever hit home runs into the center field bleachers. The stadium is slated for demolition by 1991 and a new stadium is to be built on the same site.

as it's helped me," says Jim Rice, who specializes in savage line drives that bang off The Wall but might carry into more distant seats in other parks.

Like the dimensions of ball parks, local ground rules can influence the outcome of a game as much as an umpire's call. Ted Williams lost a homer in 1941 when a drive hit the Yankee Stadium foul pole. "But the foul pole is in fair territory," he points out. Frank Robinson was lucky to play ten years in Cincinnati's Crosley Field, a fairly friendly park for right-handed hitters. But it had a huge scoreboard above the left center field fence, which was in play. Frank estimates he lost five to ten homers a year on drives off the scoreboard. "The year after I left," he says, "they drew a line across the board and counted all balls above it as home runs."

What a batter sees from the plate can also make a difference. A white baseball hurtling in against a sea of white shirts in center field could drive batters batty—as it used to in Yankee Stadium, Wrigley Field, and elsewhere. The Cardinals used to wonder why Stan Musial never hit many balls out of Sportsman's Park on Sundays or in the World Series. After 2,000 seats were roped off in center field, Stan started slugging again.

Nowadays outfields are kept empty of obstructions, but there was a time when rolled tarpaulins and storage sheds were commonly installed in fair territory, and balls hit to, over or inside them were in play. Both the Polo Grounds and Yankee Stadium had monuments in deep center field, potentially a fielder's nemesis and a long-ball hitter's salvation.

In earlier years, balls that bounced into the stands were homers; since 1931 they've been ground rule doubles. On the other hand, balls that landed

foul were considered foul, even if they passed the foul pole as fair balls. Today they are homers. We don't know how many home runs Ruth, Foxx, and others lost to one rule and gained from the other.

The record books give Hack Wilson the National League home run record with 56. It should have been 57. Cincinnati catcher Clyde Sukeforth claims that Hack "hit one in Cincinnati one day, hit so hard that it hit the screen and bounced back." The umpire thought it hit the fence below the screen and ruled it a double. "I was sitting in the Cincinnati bullpen," Sukeforth grinned, "and of course we weren't going to say anything."

But funny bounces aren't just ancient history. Modern stadiums, particularly the domes, have their own quirks. Mike Schmidt lofted a ball 117 feet high and 329 feet from home plate, hitting a speaker at the top of the Astrodome. It was ruled a single.

Whitey Ford estimates that his buddy Mickey Mantle lost an average of ten homers a year in long outs at Yankee Stadium. Bill Skowron hit only 211 homers in fourteen years, nine of them playing at home in Yankee Stadium. Skowron says, "I hit five homers and fifteen RBI in my first three games in Boston. I wish I'd played in a smaller park."

Glenn Davis of Houston estimates he loses ten homers a year at the Astrodome. "I don't think we'll ever know my true home run potential," Glenn sighs. "I'd like to see how far they could go somewhere else."

The speculation could go on and on. The truth is, in such a hodge-podge of wildly angled stadiums, yesteryear's home run records take on different meaning. Traditionalists may sneer at the monotony of today's concrete stadium architecture, but the newer ballparks have brought long overdue uniformity to the game. ◗

The Minnesota Twins' indoor, symmetrical, climate controlled, and "carpeted" Hubert H. Humphrey Metrodome in Minneapolis is not without its quirks. The 23-foot-high mylar wall in right field is rarely the source of a true carom, a nightmare to fielders but a joy to left-handed sluggers.

Measuring the Man

All Time Leaders: Batting Average

Ty Cobb
.367

Tris Speaker
.344

Ted Williams
.344

Part of the pleasure of following baseball is that old heroes never die; their achievements are enshrined in the record books to provide fuel for endless speculation about baseball's past, present and future. All measurements of batting performance begin with raw data—box scores and score cards that give the bare bones story of what actually took place on the field on a given day: who hit the home runs, who struck out, who walked, who got caught stealing, and so on. Every year the records are updated for leaders in countless categories: home runs, runs batted in, strikeouts, and walks are just the beginning.

It's this vast and, for the most part, highly accurate record of major league baseball (we have newspaper box scores for virtually every game played in the 20th century) that lets us replay last season's crucial contests, reopen old controversies, even evaluate imaginary matchups between players like Ruth and Aaron who never met on a playing field. To make sense out of all this data—to look for meaningful connections between one number and another—explains the fascination, verging on obsession, that baseball people have with statistics.

Of course, you can go back only so far, even with baseball records. In 1887, home plate was only twelve inches wide, four strikes were out, and a walk—on *five* balls—counted as a base hit. Obviously, comparing batting averages from that year with those of 1937 or 1987 would be like mixing softballs and hardballs. But since the turn of the century, baseball has been played with virtually the same rules on fields with virtually the same dimensions, except for distances to outfield fences; and fans, players, coaches and managers have been juggling statistics in an attempt to pin down the elusive factors that separate winners from losers—and the truly great.

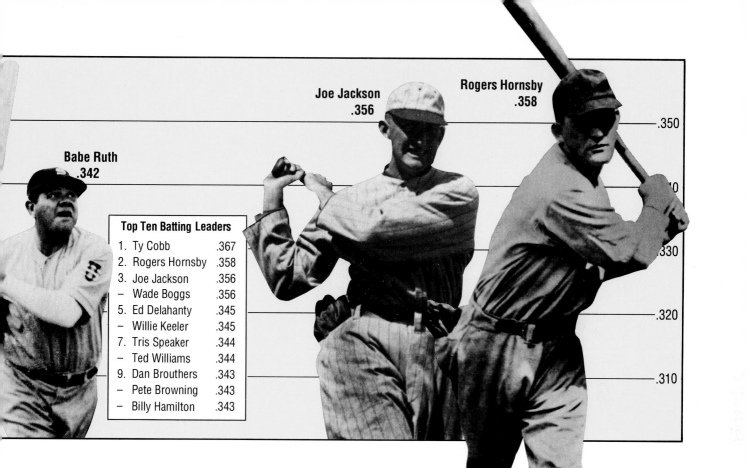

Top Ten Batting Leaders

1.	Ty Cobb	.367
2.	Rogers Hornsby	.358
3.	Joe Jackson	.356
–	Wade Boggs	.356
5.	Ed Delahanty	.345
–	Willie Keeler	.345
7.	Tris Speaker	.344
–	Ted Williams	.344
9.	Dan Brouthers	.343
–	Pete Browning	.343
–	Billy Hamilton	.343

The oldest, simplest, and most universally known batting statistic is the batting average (BA). This simple formula—total official at-bats divided by total hits—appeared in newspaper accounts of baseball games as early as 1865. At first glance, the BA seems straightforward enough. Even casual fans know that consistent .300 hitters like Wade Boggs and Don Mattingly (who get at least three hits for every ten appearances at bat) are among the game's elite, while a player who cannot keep his batting average above .200 is not long for the major leagues. The all-time batting champ is Ty Cobb, with a career BA of .367, followed by Rogers Hornsby at .358, Wade Boggs and Joe Jackson at .356, Ed Delahanty and Willie Keeler at .345, Tris Speaker and Ted Williams at .344; Babe Ruth's career record is .342.

The trouble with the batting average as a performance measurement is that it tells you nothing about the other offensive skills that help win games. Because the batting average leaves out so much, one statistician went so far as to call it "that venerable, uncannily durable fraud." For example, by counting *only* hits, the batting average does an injustice to the savvy batter who keeps a rally alive by "working" a pitcher for a walk or advances a runner with a perfectly executed sacrifice bunt. Even more unfortunate, by giving equal weight to a single and an extra-base hit, the batting average undervalues the contributions of free-swinging sluggers who strike out a lot but explode for the big one with men on base. The importance of the long ball is appreciated not only by homer-hungry fans but also by pennant-hungry owners, who pay the highest salaries to players who send balls over the fences. As pitcher Fritz Ostermueller once put it, home run hitters drive Cadillacs and singles hitters drive Fords.

If you're looking for an easy-to-calculate, easy-to-remember number that

Babe Ruth
.690

Jimmie Foxx
.609

Hank Greenberg
.605

Joe DiMaggio
.579

does a better job of ranking hitters than the batting average does, consider the slugging average (SA). This is the ratio of total *bases* to total official at-bats. By counting a home run as four bases rather than one hit, the slugging average certainly gives extra-base hitters their due. Although Pete Rose's lifetime batting average of .305 far outshines Reggie Jackson's .263, Jackson has a clear advantage in slugging average: .493 to .415. The career leader in slugging average is Babe Ruth at .690, with Ted Williams second at .634 and Lou Gehrig third at .632.

But in other ways, the SA is also flawed. It makes no allowance for bases-on-balls, sacrifices, getting picked off or caught stealing, or the number or frequency of clutch hits. If you could take *all* those other stats into account, you would certainly have a better basis for an objective comparison between, say, a Wade Boggs—who has a high batting average, strikes out infrequently, and rarely homers—and a pure slugger like Jose Canseco.

Baseball statisticians are well aware of these problems and many have risen to the challenge, inventing and justifying better performance measurements. Bill James, a veteran statistician and widely published baseball savant, once developed a formula to calculate a batter's "runs created." There's also a measurement called the "game-winning RBI." A newer and more comprehensive analytical tool is known as the "base-out percentage." Barry Codell, its inventor, calls it "baseball's most complete and informative offensive statistic." A similar version, called "total average," is espoused by noted sports columnist Thomas Boswell. On the not unreasonable assumption that scoring runs is what the game is all about, these formulas—which for convenience we can call the "base-out average"—look at *everything* a hitter does to advance himself and his teammates to home plate.

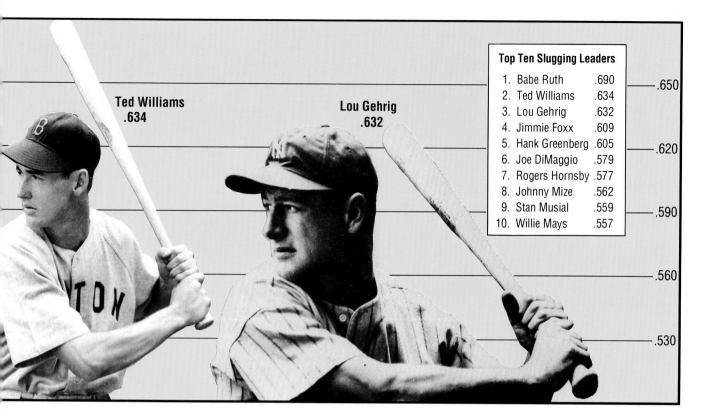

Top Ten Slugging Leaders

1.	Babe Ruth	.690
2.	Ted Williams	.634
3.	Lou Gehrig	.632
4.	Jimmie Foxx	.609
5.	Hank Greenberg	.605
6.	Joe DiMaggio	.579
7.	Rogers Hornsby	.577
8.	Johnny Mize	.562
9.	Stan Musial	.559
10.	Willie Mays	.557

Ted Williams
.634

Lou Gehrig
.632

To compute the base component of the base-out average, you add to-gether a hitter's total bases, his walks, the number of times he was hit by a pitch, his stolen bases, and (in Codell's version) his sacrifice flies and bunts. But the BOA doesn't stop there. Since even the greatest hitters are put out more often than they get on base, the BOA also considers *everything* a player does that costs his team one of the 27 outs each side is allowed per game. To determine the out component of the base-out average, you subtract a player's hits from his total at-bats, then add to the remainder his sacrifice bunts and flies, the times he was caught stealing, the double plays he grounded into, and any other outs he makes. Then simply divide his bases by his outs—and the result is the base-out average.

It sounds more complicated than it is. With a pocket calculator and a little patience, anyone can compile BOAs using raw data from an accurate score-card. A BOA of .70 means that for every seven bases a player gains for his team, he costs his team ten outs. This turns out to be about average for today's major leaguers. A BOA of .80 is quite respectable, .90 is extremely good, and 1.00 (which means a player rounds as many bases as he makes outs) is ex-traordinary. Comparing the careers of Reggie Jackson and Pete Rose, the base-out average leaves no doubt as to who was the more effective offensive player: Jackson's lifetime BOA is .86, Rose's is .75.

To verify that a new statistical yardstick like the base-out average makes sense, we can apply it to the peak achievements of great hitters. For example, to win the Triple Crown in batting, a hitter must lead his league in batting average, home runs, and runs batted in during the same year. You can argue about the relative value of the three components, but winning the Triple Crown itself is a convincingly rare feat; only 14 players in both leagues have ever had

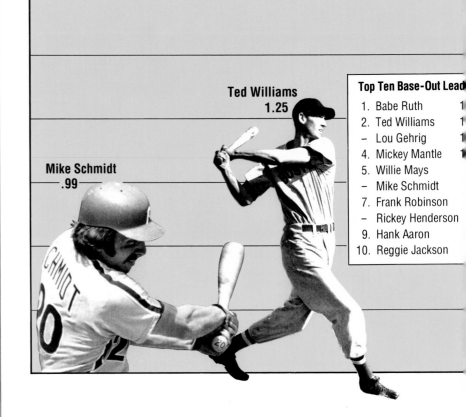

Ted Williams
1.25

Mike Schmidt
.99

Top Ten Base-Out Lead	
1. Babe Ruth	1
2. Ted Williams	1
– Lou Gehrig	1
4. Mickey Mantle	1
5. Willie Mays	
– Mike Schmidt	
7. Frank Robinson	
– Rickey Henderson	
9. Hank Aaron	
10. Reggie Jackson	

Triple Crown seasons. Carl Yastrzemski last turned the trick in 1967; he hit 44 home runs, batted in 121 runs, and had a .326 batting average—and his BOA was a healthy 1.15.

It would be fun to go back to earlier eras and see how yesterday's stars compare with current leaders in base-out averages. Unfortunately, some key statistics (such as times caught stealing and grounding into double plays) were not regularly recorded prior to 1940, so it isn't possible to compile accurate BOAs for many past greats. But if BOAs are computed on the basis of hitting records alone, the all-time leader is Babe Ruth, with a phenomenal career mark of 1.42. Ruth also has five of the six highest single-season BOAs. Close behind Ruth in career BOAs are Ted Williams and Lou Gehrig with 1.25. Mickey Mantle has a 1.10 BOA, Willie Mays a .99; Lou Brock (the career stolen-base champion) does no better than .68.

So, with all its virtues, is the base-out average on its way to being accepted as the statistic of choice for evaluating batting prowess? Don't hold your breath. Among knowledgeable baseball people, the BOA has as many critics as advocates. Critics point out that the formula assigns equal weight to a single and a walk, yet singles produce more runs; it fails to account for anomalies in home ballparks. But most of all, it ignores the fact that in the all-important category of run production, not all bases are created equal.

For the ideal stat, you'd have to decide what value to assign specific skills. How many home runs does an Eddie Murray have to hit to compensate for striking out a lot with men on base? Since a single will usually score a runner from second, a single is clearly more valuable than a walk—but exactly how much more valuable?

As you might suspect, mathematical formulas that try to account for such

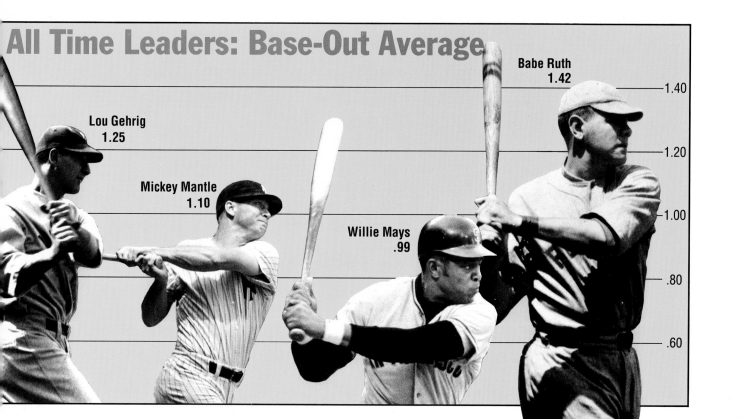

All Time Leaders: Base-Out Average

Lou Gehrig
1.25

Mickey Mantle
1.10

Willie Mays
.99

Babe Ruth
1.42

1.40

1.20

1.00

.80

.60

factors have been put forward by statisticians. If you think the base-out average is complicated, consider "linear weights" (LWTS), a formula derived by intense research and computation by former American League statistician Pete Palmer. To compile this type of stat, a "run-producing value" is assigned to every offensive event on the ball field. Underlying the LWTS system is a massive study of thousands of major league box scores that showed how many runs are produced by the average single, double, triple, homer, walk, steal, etc., and how many runs are "lost" to a team by the average out (including times caught stealing).

There are some surprises in these figures. For example, statistics compiled from thousands of box scores prove that four singles are actually more desirable than one home run; on average, four singles bring 1.8 runs across the plate, while the average home run produces 1.4 runs. Not only do four singles turn out to be more productive than one home run, but a stolen base is a lot less valuable than you might think, despite the excitement it generates in a crucial inning; in fact, it takes seven stolen bases to equal the run-producing value of the average homer.

LWTS also assigns run-producing values to such things as moving runners into scoring position for someone else to bring home and prolonging an inning to allow runners to score on hits, errors, steals, etc. An attempt has even been made to adjust the data for different home ballparks. In the name of fairness, a hitter who spends most of his career in a pitcher-friendly park (like Dodger Stadium) gets a mathematical compensation; there's an equivalent "penalty" for careers spent in hitter-friendly parks (like Wrigley Field). LWTS is not only based on a fiendishly complicated formula, but it relies on so many judgment calls to generate data that you can end up wondering just

Lou Gehrig—The Iron Horse

For 14 years, Lou Gehrig was as close to a perfect hitter as the game has ever seen, but he's remembered less for how he played than how often he played. Only a feat as incredible as Gehrig's playing in 2,130 straight games could overshadow his impact as a slugger. And only a disease as crippling as amyotrophic lateral sclerosis (ALS) could keep the man they called "The Iron Horse" from pushing the streak further. The debilitating muscle disease that killed him at age 37—and came to bear his name—also cut short a spectacular baseball career.

The object in baseball is to produce the most runs, and no player in history produced more runs per game than Gehrig. The Yankee first baseman drove in .92 runs per game—tying him for first in that category with Detroit's Sam Crawford and Hank Greenberg—and scored .87 runs per game, 11th all time. From 1926 to 1938, Gehrig was a phenomenal slugger, hitting .343 and averaging 36 home runs, 137 RBI, 139 runs scored, 39 doubles, 12 triples, 112 walks, and just 56 strikeouts per season. The more runners on base, the better Gehrig liked it, as evidenced by his record 23 grand slams, including three in a four-game stretch in 1931. Gehrig's feat of seven seasons of 150 or more RBI has never been equalled. In addition, he averaged 1.77 RBI per home run, tops among players with 300 or more home runs.

The son of German immigrants, Gehrig was the only one of their four children to survive to adulthood. He was an excellent all-around athlete in high school and enrolled at Columbia University in 1921 on a football scholarship, although he soon became known more for the titanic home runs he bounced off campus buildings. Gehrig left Columbia after just two years to sign with the Yankees. After brief but memorable appearances with the Yankees in 1923 and 1924—he hit .447 in 23 games—Gehrig was in the majors to stay in 1925. On June 1 an appearance as a pinch hitter officially started the consecutive-game streak, although more remember the following game, when Gehrig replaced Wally Pipp in the starting lineup; he remained the Yankee starting first baseman for the next 14 years.

Gehrig exploded in 1927 for 47 homers and 175 RBI as the clean-up hitter on what many consider the best team ever. The Yankees swept the Pirates in the World Series, and Gehrig was named the league's Most Valuable Player. In the 1928 World Series, the Yankees swept the Cardinals as Gehrig hit .545 with four homers and nine RBI. In World Series play, Gehrig ranks among the top ten career batters in every offensive category.

Gehrig's amazing run production continued into the next decade, as he drove in 174 runs in 1930 and set the American League mark of 184 RBI in 1931. In 1932 "Columbia Lou" became only the third man in history to hit four home runs in a single game. Then, in the 1932 World Series, he batted .529 with three homers and eight RBI as the Yankees swept the Cubs. Gehrig won the Triple Crown in 1934 with a .363 average, 49 homers, and 165 RBI, and with Joe DiMaggio led the Yankees to three consecutive world championships from 1936 to 1938.

LOU
GEHRIG

First Base
New York Yankees 1923-1939
Hall of Fame 1939

GAMES	2,164
AT BATS	8,001
BATTING AVERAGE	
Career	.340
Season High	.379
BATTING TITLES	**1934**
SLUGGING AVERAGE	
Career *(3rd all time)*	.632
Season High *(4th all time)*	.765
HITS	
Career	2,721
Season High	220
DOUBLES	
Career	535
Season High	52
TRIPLES	
Career	162
Season High	20
HOME RUNS	
Career	493
Season High	49
TOTAL BASES	5,059
(10th all time)	
EXTRA BASE HITS	1,190
(5th all time)	
RUNS BATTED IN	
Career *(3rd all time)*	1,990
Season High *(2nd all time)*	184
RUNS	
Career *(7th all time)*	1,888
Season High *(4th all time)*	167
WORLD SERIES	1926-1928
	1932, 1936-1938
MOST VALUABLE PLAYER	
	1927, 1936

In 1938—Gehrig's last full season—he played on his sixth world championship Yankee team.

In 1938 Gehrig's production dropped off: although he hit 29 homers and drove in 114 runs, he hit below .300 for the first time since 1925. By spring training in 1939, it was clear something was physically wrong with Gehrig. After batting .143 in the regular season's first eight games, Gehrig took himself out of the lineup and the streak was broken. Reporters and fans offered numerous theories on the demise of Gehrig's skills, from gallbladder trouble to brain tumors to self-doubt. But on June 19 a press release from the Mayo Clinic confirmed the diagnosis of ALS.

Gehrig stayed with the Yankees as a nonplaying captain for the rest of the 1939 season and brought his usual grace and geniality to his new role on the bench. "So help me, for 15 years I never saw a ballgame as it should be watched," he said. "I never appreciated some of the fellows I've been playing with for years. What I always thought were routine plays when I was in the lineup are really thrilling when you see 'em from off the field."

By 1941 the disease had rendered Gehrig, an outstanding physical specimen who had played through broken fingers, back pain, beanings, and countless minor bumps and bruises, unable to dress or feed himself. On June 2, 1941, two weeks before his 38th birthday, Lou Gehrig died, 16 years to the day after replacing Pipp as the Yankees' starting first baseman.

what the final numbers mean. For instance, it's no surprise that the all-time batting champion according to LWTS is Babe Ruth—*unless* you make an adjustment for the five wartime years that Ted Williams missed because of military service, in which case Williams beats out Ruth, *unless* you take into account Ruth's years as a pitcher, in which case. . . . Well, you get the idea.

Despite its acknowledged subjective bias, the Most Valuable Player award, given annually in both the American and National leagues, is baseball's ultimate accolade. It is the one award for which both pitchers and position players are eligible. The award is intended to recognize a player's total contribution to the team.

Awards for excellence on the diamond have been given annually, in one form or another, as far back as 1875, although the Chalmers Award is generally recognized as the first "official" Most Valuable Player award. Awarded by Hugh Chalmers, president of the Chalmers Motor Company, the award was first given in 1910 to the player with the highest batting average. The subjective element was introduced in 1911, when the Chalmers Award—and a Chalmers "30" automobile—was awarded to the player who contributed the most to his team in the opinion of baseball writers from each major league city. Discontinued in 1914, the Chalmers Award was followed from 1922 to 1929 by the League Awards, which were presented and overseen by the American and National leagues. Since 1931, the Baseball Writers Association of America (BWAA) has administered the MVP for both leagues. Voting is limited to two sportswriters selected for each team in each major league city.

It's not surprising that over the years writers have looked to pennant-winning teams for their MVP choices. But that has not always been the case,

Though computers have replaced scorecards, the team statistician—half math professor, half baseball fan—plays as important a role as ever in compiling the new, more sophisticated measurements of productivity.

While a successful sacrifice bunt has no effect on a player's batting and slugging averages, it can improve his base-out average. Minnesota pitcher Les Straker (opposite) had never been to bat in the major leagues before the 1987 World Series, and it showed.

Hitting into double plays is hard on a player's base-out average, since it counts as two outs as opposed to one in batting and slugging averages.

A minor league slugger with major league aspirations, the Mets' John Gibbons got more attention than at-bats in the majors. Gibbons (above) set a Class AAA Tidewater record with five career grand slams, but managed just 50 at-bats and one homer in parts of four seasons in the big leagues.

as fans of the Chicago Cubs know only too well. In 1952, Hank Sauer, league leader in home runs and RBI, won the award with the fifth-place Cubs. Six years later, the Cubs' Ernie Banks won the first of his two awards—1958 and 1959—although in neither year did the Cubs finish either in the first division or above .500. In 1958, Banks hit .313 and led the league with 47 homers and 129 RBI; the following year he hit .304 with 45 home runs and 143 RBI.

When the MVP is not a runaway, as it was in the American League in 1988 when the Oakland Athletics' Jose Canseco became the twelfth player ever to win the award by unanimous vote, it's frequently a two-horse race, with the deciding factor frequently involving record-breaking performances. In 1961 Mickey Mantle hit .317 with 54 homers and 128 RBI but was beaten out for the MVP award by teammate Roger Maris, who broke Ruth's home run record and drove in a league-leading 142 RBI, although he batted only .269. But there are no rules to human nature: when Ruth broke his own home run record in 1927, Lou Gehrig beat out the Babe for MVP.

The classic contest took place in 1941. Joe DiMaggio batted .357 with 30 home runs and a league-leading 125 RBI. Ted Williams led the league with 37 HR and a spectacular .406 average, while driving in 120 runs. But the Yankees finished 17 games ahead of the Red Sox and went on to defeat the Brooklyn Dodgers in the World Series. DiMaggio walked away with the MVP honors by 37 points over Williams, perhaps because DiMaggio picked that year to hit safely in 56 consecutive games.

In the end, the point of baseball, as of all games, is to win—and the purpose of baseball statistics and awards is to help players, coaches, scouts, managers and fans better understand the contributions that each player, no matter how individually talented, makes to his team's success. ⬤

MEASURING MICKEY HATCHER

To see how various performance measurements compare, consider Dodger outfielder Mickey Hatcher. Hatcher hit .293 in 1988—second best on the team—but his slugging average was barely mediocre at .351, and since he rarely walks, his base-out average was downright lousy at .53. But in the World Series, Hatcher was, by any measurable standard, a true slugger.

To determine Hatcher's World Series batting average, simply divide his hits—seven—by his at-bats—19. The result is .368, a clip that, were he able to sustain it for an entire season, would likely have earned Hatcher his first batting title.

Hatcher's slugging average—computed by dividing his total bases into his at-bats—is even more impressive. Hatcher had two homers, one double, and four singles, for a total of 14 bases; divided by 19 official at-bats, that gives him a .737 slugging average. Had Hatcher kept that mark up all season, it would have been the ninth best of all time.

To get Hatcher's base-out average, add walks, sacrifices, stolen bases, and times hit by pitch to his total bases. Hatcher walked once in the Series and had no sacrifices or steals, nor was he hit by a pitch, so he had 15 total bases. The other part of the equation is the number of outs, sacrifices, and times caught stealing. He made 12 outs—20 total at-bats minus seven hits and one walk—had no sacrifices and was not caught stealing. Divide 15 by 12 and Hatcher's base-out average is 1.25—a Lou Gehrig-style pace.

Hatcher's 1988 World Series

	ab	1b	2b	3b	hr	sb	cs	bb	sac	hp
Total	19	4	1	0	2	0	0	1	0	0

Batting Avg.	.368 (7 hits in 19 at-bats)
Slugging Avg.	.737 (14 bases in 19 at-bats)
Base-Out Avg.	1.25 (15 bases, 12 outs)

Jimmie Foxx

There were two ways to measure the greatness of Jimmie Foxx—by his strength and by his numbers. Affectionately called "The Beast" by teammates, Foxx built up his muscles lifting bales of hay on his father's farm in Sudlersville, Maryland, then used them to batter major league pitching for two decades. Yankee pitcher Lefty Gomez liked to say that even Jimmie Foxx's hair had muscles. Foxx stood six feet tall and weighed a solid 195 pounds, and when he stood at home plate in his sleeveless jersey his biceps would ripple. "He wasn't born," Gomez once said. "He was trapped."

Foxx, in all his strength, was one of the most intimidating hitters in the game. His tape measure home runs are legendary: he is one of the few men to hit a ball into the third deck in left field at Yankee Stadium. Twice he hit balls completely out of Chicago's Comiskey Park. Ruth did it only once. Foxx's strength was so respected that he received six consecutive walks in a single game.

Foxx's Boston Red Sox teammate Ted Williams said that when Foxx "hit one it sounded like an explosion." And in 1932 Foxx exploded all season long. Only a nagging wrist injury and two new ballpark screens kept him from breaking Babe Ruth's five-year-old record of 60 homers in a season. On July 19, Foxx hit his 30th homer and was 32 days ahead of Ruth's 1927 pace. He wound up with 58, although records show he hit nine balls against screens in Cleveland and St. Louis that weren't there when Ruth set his mark. To go with the 58 homers, Foxx added a .364 batting average, 213 hits, 151 runs scored, 169 RBI, and a .749 slugging average, the seventh best single season slugging average ever.

Appropriately enough, Foxx was discovered by Frank "Home Run" Baker, himself a Marylander. In 1924 Baker convinced Philadelphia Athletics manager Connie Mack to sign the 18-year-old Foxx. In 1925 Foxx got just nine at-bats—all as a pinch hitter—and hit safely six times. That six-for-nine performance was the beginning of a professional career that was consistently filled with phenomenal numbers. Foxx's list of accomplishments includes four home run titles, three RBI crowns, and five slugging average titles. As the American League's Most Valuable Player in 1932, 1933 and 1938, he was the first of six players to win the award three times. He was the youngest player to hit 500 home runs, reaching that milestone at age 33. And he homered when it counted, averaging 1.76 RBI per home run, best among the top ten all-time home run leaders.

Foxx came up as a catcher, but no one—not even Jimmie Foxx—was ready to replace future Hall of Famer Mickey Cochrane behind the plate. In his first four years in the majors, Foxx was used sparingly, but in 1927 Mack finally found a place to put his young slugger—first base. Two years later Foxx led the Athletics to the American League pennant, hitting .354 with 33 homers and 117 RBI. His

JIMMIE FOXX

First Base
Philadelphia Athletics 1925-1935
Boston Red Sox 1936-1942
Chicago Cubs 1942-1944
Philadelphia Phillies 1945
Hall of Fame 1951

GAMES	**2,317**
AT BATS	**8,134**
BATTING AVERAGE	
Career	**.325**
Season High	**.364**
BATTING TITLES	**1933, 1938**
SLUGGING AVERAGE	
Career *(4th all time)*	**.609**
Season High *(7th all time)*	**.749**
HITS	
Career	**2,646**
Season High	**213**
DOUBLES	
Career	**458**
Season High	**37**
TRIPLES	
Career	**125**
Season High	**13**
HOME RUNS	
Career *(9th all time)*	**534**
Season High *(3rd all time)*	**58**
TOTAL BASES	**4,956**
EXTRA BASE HITS	**1,117**
(10th all time)	
RUNS BATTED IN	
Career *(6th all time)*	**1,921**
Season High *(4th all time)*	**175**
RUNS	
Career	**1,751**
Season High	**151**
WORLD SERIES	**1929, 1930**
	1931
MOST VALUABLE PLAYER	
	1932, 1933, 1938

The strongest player of his time, Foxx regularly swung four bats to warm up.

two homers provided the winning margin in the first two games of the World Series, and the Athletics went on to beat the Cubs in five games. That season was the start of one of the greatest slugging accomplishments in history: an unprecedented string of 12 straight 30-plus home run seasons for "Double X." Foxx's numbers continued to pile up over the course of a 20-year career. When he retired in 1945, Foxx had put together a .325 career batting average. His 534 lifetime homers rank ninth on the all-time list; his 1,921 RBI rank sixth; and his .609 slugging percentage is the fourth best ever.

During his marvelous 1932 season, Foxx's .364 batting average was just .003 short of bringing him the Triple Crown. That was not the case the following season, when he led the American League with a .356 average, 48 homers, and 163 RBI. Foxx also tied a major league record by homering in four consecutive at-bats in June 1933.

Philadelphia had a splendid team, with Hall of Famers Cochrane, Al Simmons, and Lefty Grove to go with Foxx, and the Athletics won pennants in 1930 and 1931. But at the end of the 1932 season, Connie Mack, manager and owner of the ballclub, did as he had in 1914 and dismantled a great team by selling off its stars for cash. Simmons, third base-

man Jimmy Dykes, and outfielder Mule Haas were sold to the White Sox for $100,000, and Cochrane went a year later to Detroit for another $100,000. Even though Foxx was rumored to have signed for just $18,000 in 1934 and was the most popular of the Athletics, Mack cashed him in in the winter of 1935 for $150,000 from Red Sox owner Tom Yawkey.

The right-handed Foxx feasted on Fenway Park's short left field wall, averaging 40 homers per season from 1936 to 1940. In 1938, he won another batting title with a .349 average, another RBI title with 175—the fourth highest single season total ever—and hit 50 home runs, as the Red Sox climbed into second place.

Like many other 1930s sluggers, Foxx liked to drink, and by 1942 too much alcohol, too many late nights, and a chronic sinus condition had diminished his skills. He was waived by Boston and picked up by the Chicago Cubs. Foxx ended his playing career in 1945 with the Phillies, then managed in the minor leagues for a few years.

Obscured by his awesome power and talent as a hitter were Foxx's ability and versatility in the field. As a first baseman, he led the American League in fielding average three times. But because Mack had a hard time figuring out where to play

While Phillie catcher Jimmie Wilson looks on, Jimmie Foxx accepts congratulations from teammate Bob Johnson for Foxx's only All-Star Game home run —a two-run, first inning shot in 1935. The American League defeated the National League 4–1 in Cleveland.

him early in his career, Foxx grew accustomed to playing wherever he was needed. In 1928—his first full season—he split his time between first base, third base, and catcher, and in 13 of the next 15 seasons played at least two positions. Foxx's vote totals for the 1933 All-Star Game showed that fans thought highly of his skills, but that many weren't sure what position he played. Foxx garnered 271,508 votes—seventh highest among American League players—but he didn't get enough at any one position to gain a starting role. He did get 891 votes at second base—the only infield position he never played in his career. Foxx even excelled as a pitcher. In 1945 he compiled a 1.59 earned-run average, allowing just 13 hits in $22\frac{2}{3}$ innings with the Phillies.

One of the most popular players among his teammates, Foxx fell on hard times after he left baseball. His income had increased considerably when he joined the Red Sox, and so had his spending habits. "He was always grabbing for the check," Williams said. "Poor Jimmie, he never thought the money would stop coming in." Foxx's business ventures all failed, and he drifted from job to job. Elected to the Hall of Fame in 1951, Foxx died on July 21, 1967, at the age of 60.

The Power Game

he year was 1987, the year of the homer—a record-breaking 4,458 of them. Seventy-eight players hit 20 or more home runs; 27 players topped the 30 mark. In terms of muscle, in terms of sheer power, 1987 is unprecedented in baseball history: *everyone* was swinging for the fences, and 25,099 strikeouts remain in the record book to prove it.

The power barrage of 1987 was a phenomenon with nearly as many explanations as homers. Most folks, including some physicists, blamed the ball—which was livelier than ever, they claimed, though test after test failed to provide conclusive evidence of any kind. Some said it was the bats, that players were loading them up or hollowing them out. Sports physiologists stood by the argument that scientific conditioning, new methods of weight training, and maybe even the wonders of chemistry made sluggers stronger than ever. Old-timers blamed the pitchers, accusing them of cowardice, and pitchers blamed a shallower strike zone. In fact, 1987 was just one of those years—a long time coming and with much forewarning.

It all started with 60 homers 60 years before, when Babe Ruth eclipsed his own single-season record of 59 home runs. For nearly a decade, baseball purists had blamed the home run for spoiling what the game of baseball was meant to be. Year after year, homers were being hit in record numbers, although the 1927 total of 922 is but a scratch single compared to the slugging output 60 years later. Suddenly, runs were crossing the plate in such numbers that they seemed undeserved—in a sense *unearned*. Whereas the home run

Oakland first baseman Mark McGwire hit 49 home runs in 1987, shattering the all-time rookie record of 38.

Lou Gehrig was the
Yankee clean-up hitter
behind Ruth from
1925 to 1934. Modest
and reserved, Gehrig
brought respectability
to slugging.

1987: A Great Year For The Long Ball

Who's to say if the bats were loaded or if there really was a rabbit inside the ball? By season's end, more homers than ever had been hit, and a record 27 players hit 30 or more homers.

The 30-Plus Club, 1987

Player	Team	HR	Player	Team	HR
1. Andre Dawson	Chicago, NL	49	15. Cory Snyder	Cleveland	33
– Mark McGwire	Oakland	49	16. Tom Brunansky	Minnesota	32
3. George Bell	Toronto	47	– Joe Carter	Cleveland	32
4. Dale Murphy	Atlanta	44	– Brook Jacoby	Cleveland	32
5. Darryl Strawberry	New York, NL	39	– Matt Nokes	Detroit	32
6. Eric Davis	Cincinnati	37	– Mike Pagliarulo	New York, AL	32
7. Howard Johnson	New York, NL	36	– Larry Parrish	Texas	32
8. Jack Clark	St. Louis	35	22. Jose Canseco	Oakland	31
– Will Clark	San Francisco	35	– Gary Gaetti	Minnesota	31
10. Darrell Evans	Detroit	34	– Larry Sheets	Baltimore	31
– Dwight Evans	Boston	34	25. Don Mattingly	New York, AL	30
– Wally Joyner	California	34	– Eddie Murray	Baltimore	30
– Kent Hrbek	Minnesota	34	– Ruben Sierra	Texas	30
– Danny Tartabull	Kansas City	34			

was once the domain of Ruth only—as in 1919, when the Babe hit a record-breaking 29 round trippers and no more than five other players hit as many as 12—1927 was a bit more democratic. Ruth's teammates Lou Gehrig and Tony Lazzeri hit 47 and 18 home runs, respectively, while in the National League Chicago's Hack Wilson and Philadelphia's Cy Williams each hit 30. Once again, the lively ball was held accountable.

The home run tally of 1927 was only a hint of the numbers to come, particularly those of the 1950s through the 1980s. But 1927 began the trend and, perhaps just as importantly, legitimized sheer power as a viable strategic weapon. In the years of prohibition, when *temperance* was at least the official byword, Ruth and the home run stood for excess on and off the field. Homers and high times were always within his reach, and the fans approved.

Laboring in Ruth's shadow, though not out of the spotlight, was the great Lou Gehrig, who hit 493 career home runs. "Columbia Lou," perhaps more than anyone else, made the home run acceptable to baseball purists. In the words of baseball historian David Voigt, Gehrig was "the Galahad of the era." He was educated, reserved and polite; in short, his manner was everything Ruth's was not. Gehrig's slugging success, modest by Ruthian standards, was impressive: in 1925, his first full season with the Yankees, Gehrig hit 20 home runs in 126 games; the following year he hit 16 in 155 games.

Then 1927 happened. Gehrig batted .373, drove in 175 runs, and hit ten more homers than he'd previously hit in his entire career. Anyone who watched Gehrig play that season sensed that 1927 was not a "career year" but a promise of years to come. Gehrig's 47 home runs—more than anyone but Ruth had ever hit in a single season—suddenly made the round tripper legitimate. After all, Lou was "a college man," though he sure didn't hit like

A Hall of Fame outfielder for the Chicago Cubs, Hack Wilson started as a catcher in 1920 for a team in Eddystone, Pennsylvania. By 1926 he had become part of baseball's power surge.

Catcher Mickey Cochrane (above, right) could beat you with his bat, his glove, or his intense will to win. Cochrane played in five World Series in his 13-year career with the Athletics and Tigers. "Winning was a way of life with him," said Detroit slugger Hank Greenberg.

one. Gehrig was proof that a good and upright lad could fit in to the home run craze and survive very well.

For the next 60 years, the strategic significance of power in general, and the home run in particular, became more and more deeply ingrained in the game. The totals of stolen bases plunged and homers soared in record numbers. There were landmark years in landmark eras in which home run records were shattered and previously inconceivable new standards set. Not even Babe Ruth, the most imaginative ballplayer ever, could have dreamed how much and how often his power charged and recharged the game during the next six decades.

Y ou'd have to travel to a different planet to match a year like 1930, which was unquestionably the year of the hitter. The National League batting average was .303. Six National League teams hit .300 or better, with the Giants leading the majors at a .319 clip. The league's 892 home runs were just 30 homers shy of what both leagues hit in 1927, baseball's previous milestone season. The Phillies' Chuck Klein batted .386 on 250 hits, including 40 home runs, and drove in 170 runs; he finished no higher than second in any of the four categories. And Hack Wilson and Bill Terry were the reasons why. Wilson set major league and National League records with 190 RBI and 56 home runs, respectively; Terry led all hitters with a .401 average on 254 hits. Wilson and Klein were followed in the home run department by Wally Berger of the Boston Braves, Gabby Hartnett of the Cubs, and Babe Herman of the Dodgers, who hit 38, 37 and 35 homers, in that order.

In the American League, Ruth and Gehrig ran a customary one-two in

*Center fielder Earl Averill suffered from
playing ten years on Cleveland Indian
teams that never finished higher than
third place. His talent and numbers are
among the best of all time.*

home runs, with 49 for the Babe and 41 for "Larrupin' Lou." Jimmie Foxx and Al Simmons were equally as formidable with the first-place Philadelphia Athletics. Foxx hit .335 with 37 homers and 156 RBI; teammate Simmons hit 36 round trippers, drove in 165 runs, and led the league in batting with a .381 average. Goose Goslin of the sixth-place St. Louis Browns chipped in with 37 home runs.

Ruth's last year with the Yankees was 1934, and he retired as an active player after just 28 games with the Boston Braves in 1935. But homers continued to pile up in his absence. Although Americans would never forget the Babe and his exploits, the new sluggers grew to heroic proportion, in part through the medium of radio, which carried games—live broadcasts and delayed studio re-creations complete with simulated background noise—from one coast to another. By the end of the decade, Mel Ott, Rip Collins, Joe Medwick, Johnny Mize, Dolf Camilli, Harlond Clift, Earl Averill, Hal Trotsky, Rudy York, Hank Greenberg, Zeke Bonura, Bob Johnson, Joe Gordon, and Bill Dickey were more than home-team favorites. They were heroes who lived along the airwaves and in the imaginations of countless fans from sandlot to sandlot across the country.

The increase in homers and radio's growing popularity were hardly coincidental. By 1930, radio was the most popular form of entertainment in the country. For one thing, listeners didn't have to buy tickets, which mattered during the Depression. But there was also something quite magical about the combination of radio and baseball. The excitement and drama of the moment—which in a home run is everything—was instantly created in the voices of announcers such as Graham McNamee, Fred Hoey, Ty Tyson, and Red Barber, who seemed able to put fans closer to the action than any box seat.

Tiger Stadium

For 87 years the Detroit Tigers have played baseball at the corner of Michigan and Trumbull. During that time, the stadiums they've played in have been renovated, expanded, renamed, belatedly lit and even wheeled around 90 degrees, but rarely have hitters complained.

What is now Tiger Stadium started out as Bennett Park, an 8,500-seat arena on the site of Detroit's old Haymarket. Named for Charley Bennett, a popular 19th century Tiger catcher, the park was the setting for Tiger World Series losses in 1907, 1908 and 1909. Seating capacity was increased to 14,000 in 1911. The Tigers' popularity caused them to outgrow Bennett Park shortly after its expansion, and besides, the afternoon sun shone directly in hitters' eyes, although it didn't seem to bother Ty Cobb, who hit .420 in Bennett Park's last season.

The sun became the right fielder's problem in 1913 as 23,000-seat Navin Field made its debut with right field where home plate used to be. In 1924 a second deck was added from first to third base, raising capacity to 29,000. In 1936 a second deck in right field increased seating to 36,000, and in 1938 new owner Walter Briggs added decks in left and center. Renamed Briggs Stadium, the park held 58,000 fans and featured a mammoth scoreboard atop the center field stands. In 1948 Briggs Stadium became the last AL park to install lights, and in 1961 it was renamed Tiger Stadium by new owner John Fetzer.

Throughout all the renovations and name changes, the concrete and steel park remained a hitter's paradise, home to greats like Cobb, Harry Heilmann, Hank Greenberg, and Al Kaline; Ted Williams called it the finest hitting park in baseball. The wind is kept out by second-deck enclosures on all sides, and a dark green background makes it easy for hitters to pick up the ball. Although its 440-foot center field is now the deepest in the majors, its power alleys are invitingly short. Even more enticing is the right-field porch, which is 325 feet from home with a second-deck overhang that is ten feet closer. With outfield fences just nine feet high, Tiger Stadium is consistently at or near the top of parks in annual home run totals.

Tiger Stadium has been the site of many momentous hitting feats. In 1941 Williams produced one of the most thrilling finishes in All-Star Game history when, with two out and two on in the bottom of the ninth and the American League trailing 5–4, he blasted a three-run homer into the second deck in right center. As a rookie, Williams hit the first of 19 homers to clear the right field roof. Tiger Stadium played host to Babe Ruth's 700th homer in 1934.

Tiger Stadium has also seen its share of the unusual over the years. In the sixth inning of Game 7 of the 1934 World Series, St. Louis's Joe Medwick slid hard into third base and tussled with Detroit's Marv Owen. When Medwick returned to left field the next inning with the Cardinals ahead 9–0, frustrated Tiger fans pelted Medwick with overripe produce. Cleaning it up just brought more crops down on Medwick's head, and to restore order Commissioner Kenesaw Mountain Landis ordered Medwick to leave the game. The Cardinals won 11–0. Lou Gehrig's consecutive game streak ended there at 2,130 on May 2, 1939.

Tiger Stadium underwent another extensive renovation—this one with an $18 million price tag in the late 1970s, and a new 30-year lease seemed to guarantee extension of Tiger Stadium's life into the 21st century. But in 1988 its future was in jeopardy as questions about structural soundness spawned talk of building a new stadium. Should it be destroyed, just Wrigley Field and Fenway Park would remain from the list of 15 concrete and steel parks built between 1909 and 1923.

Tiger Stadium's center field flag pole (above) is the highest in-play obstacle—125 feet—in the history of baseball. The stadium's official address is Michigan and Trumbull (below), but it is also bounded by Al Kaline Drive and Mickey Cochrane Avenue.

Tiger Stadium

Michigan and Trumbull Avenues
Detroit, Michigan

Built 1912

Detroit Tigers, AL
1912- Present

Seating Capacity 52,806

Style
Grass surface, asymmetrical, permanent baseball

Height of Outfield Fences
9 feet, foul pole to foul pole

Dugouts
Home: 3rd base
Visitors: 1st base

Bullpens
Recessed
Home: Left field line
Visitors: Right field line

440
365   370
340   325
66

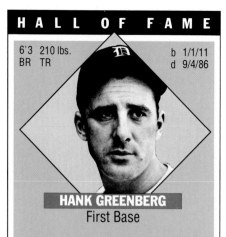

6'3 210 lbs.
BR TR

b 1/1/11
d 9/4/86

HANK GREENBERG
First Base

At age 19, Hank Greenberg turned down what was probably the dream of most boys who grew up in New York—a chance to play with the Yankees. Greenberg, a native of the Bronx, was as thoughtful as he was talented and determined. Realizing that Lou Gehrig would be the Yankee first baseman for at least ten years, Greenberg turned down an offer from the Yankees, signed instead with Detroit, and went on to have what was probably the greatest 9½-year career in the history of baseball.

The first major leaguer drafted into World War II, he lost 4½ seasons to the war. But in his nine full seasons he was a dominant slugger, winning four home run and RBI titles, and powering Detroit to four pennants and two world championships.

In 1934—his first full season—Greenberg hit .339 with an eyepopping 63 doubles, the fourth best single-season total. In 1935 he led the Tigers to their second straight pennant with 36 homers and 170 RBI.

A broken wrist cut Greenberg's 1936 season short, but in 1937 he had 183 RBI—one short of Gehrig's AL record. In 1938 Greenberg hit 58 homers—two short of Babe Ruth's mark—and tied Jimmie Foxx for the most ever by a right-handed hitter.

Greenberg's most telling statistic is his .92 RBI per game—tied for first all-time with Gehrig and Sam Crawford. Teammate Charlie Gehringer, a man of few words, said of Greenberg: "Hank loved to drive those runs in."

Joe "D" and The Kid, 1939-1951

		BA	SA	RBI	Hits	HR	2B	3B	Runs	BB
1939	DiMaggio	**.381**	.671	126	176	30	32	6	108	52
	Williams	.327	.609	**145**	185	31	44	11	131	107
1940	DiMaggio	**.352**	.626	133	179	31	28	9	93	61
	Williams	.344	.594	113	193	23	43	14	**134**	96
1941	DiMaggio	.357	.643	**125**	193	30	43	11	122	76
	Williams	**.406**	**.735**	120	185	**37**	33	3	**135**	**145**
1942	DiMaggio	.305	.498	114	186	21	29	13	123	68
	Williams	**.356**	**.648**	**137**	186	**36**	34	5	**141**	**145**
1943-1945				Military Service						
1946	DiMaggio	.290	.511	95	146	25	20	8	81	59
	Williams	.342	**.667**	123	176	38	37	8	**142**	**156**
1947	DiMaggio	.315	.522	97	168	20	31	10	97	64
	Williams	**.343**	**.634**	**114**	181	**32**	40	9	**125**	**162**
1948	DiMaggio	.320	.598	**155**	190	**39**	26	11	110	67
	Williams	**.369**	.615	127	188	25	**44**	3	124	**126**
1949	DiMaggio	.346	.596	67	94	14	14	6	58	55
	Williams	.343	**.650**	**159**	194	**43**	**39**	3	**150**	**162**
1950	DiMaggio	.301	.585	122	158	32	33	10	114	80
	Williams	.317	.647 *	97	106	28	24	1	82	82
1951	DiMaggio	.263	.422	71	109	12	22	4	72	61
	Williams	.318	**.556**	126	169	30	28	4	109	**144**

Boldface league leader
*Williams' 334 official at-bats did not qualify for batting/slugging championships.

Until the Giants and Dodgers moved from New York to California in 1958, there were never more than two big league teams west of the Mississippi River, but from coast to coast the game and its sluggers lived.

The 1930s was also the decade in which two native Californians, Joe DiMaggio and Ted Williams, made their way east to win fame in the American League as the legends of their time, as well as for a good number of years to come. They were rivals, both as idols and as players—DiMaggio with the Yankees and Williams with the Red Sox. Though no one would ever supplant the Babe in terms of stature, Williams and DiMaggio added a new, personal dimension to the slugger's star status.

There was something inscrutable about each one. Neither was a particularly public man, although being in the public eye was unavoidable, given what each could do with a bat. And their public faces were really the creations of their fans, reflections of how each man played the game. DiMaggio was the complete player, the epitome of grace; he made everything about the game—running, throwing, hitting—look easy. In 1936, his first year in the majors, DiMaggio hit .323 with 29 homers and 125 RBI, a pace he maintained for the next 12 seasons. DiMaggio became the ideal. Williams may well be the greatest hitter who ever lived; he was certainly the smartest. He was tough minded about his work, all business at the plate. His nickname: "Teddy Ballgame." When Williams broke in with the Red Sox in 1939 he was already a better hitter than virtually every player in the majors; it was a position he never relinquished. He hit .327 that season with 31 home runs and a league-leading 145 RBI. Twenty-one years, 18 big league seasons, and two wars later, Williams, age 42, hit .316 with 29 home runs. Fittingly, he homered in his final at-bat in the major leagues.

No two players have been compared more often or intensely than Red Sox left fielder Ted Williams and Yankee center fielder Joe DiMaggio, the top sluggers of their era. Williams had better individual numbers but played in just one World Series. DiMaggio played in ten.

Ted Williams' plight typified that of many players during World War II, as the Boston slugger gave up three years of his prime to the U.S. Navy. Unlike many others, Williams—a fighter pilot—also served two years in the Korean War.

Between them, DiMaggio and Williams won five American League Most Valuable Player awards. But their true value to their respective clubs was immeasurable in terms of the everyday player. They were incomparable; to speak of the greatness of one evoked the greatness of the other. Which was the case in 1941, a milestone year in slugging history. That was the season of DiMaggio's 56-game hitting streak, of Williams' .406 batting average. No major leaguer since has come close to matching either performance.

The DiMaggio and Williams slugging feats of 1941 proved to be the last until after World War II. The fate of many players involved the war in Europe. The influence of World War II on major league baseball was apparent from the very beginning of the decade; in 1940, Detroit's Hank Greenberg became the first major leaguer drafted. Two months after Williams' climactic 1941 season, the United States went to war.

Home run production fell off drastically during the war years, as virtually every team in the majors fielded teams with depleted rosters. In 1943, the leagues hit a 17-year low of 905 homers, and the Yankees were the only team to hit 100 home runs, the first time since 1926 that only one team in the majors reached that mark. For the most part, the 1940s served as a transitional era between two explosive but very different decades. The 1930s opened with Ruth still a power force with the Yankees, whereas no important longball hitter who played in the 1950s saw action during Ruth's career. The early 1940s were a dress rehearsal for the kind of slugging that would set the tone for the postwar years.

Hardly noticed amid the clamor surrounding DiMaggio's streak and Williams' .406 average was the debut of a young St. Louis Cardinal out-

Even as a skinny 21-year-old rookie in 1939, Williams had a powerful, fluid swing.

fielder/first baseman. Called up at the end of the season, 20-year-old Stan Musial appeared in just 12 games but managed 20 hits, one home run, and a .426 average. The next year he hit .315 as the Cardinals' regular right fielder. Despite his overall ability—in his first five seasons he led the league in hits and doubles three times and twice won the NL batting crown—Musial was not an overpowering home run hitter. At least not until 1948, when he hit 39 home runs and finished second to leaders Ralph Kiner of Pittsburgh and New York's Johnny Mize. Musial had come up one home run shy of sweeping every NL hitting statistic that season, as he led the league with 230 hits, 46 doubles, 18 triples, 135 runs, 131 RBI, a .376 average, and a .702 slugging percentage. During his 22-year career with the Cardinals, Musial hit .331 with 475 homers, ranking in the top ten of all time in hits, doubles, runs, RBI, walks, and slugging average. What Musial brought to the power game was a dimension beyond Williams' genius and DiMaggio's completeness: he was perhaps the greatest natural athlete of his time and one of the most durable. He became the prototype for a slugger the game would not see for another 40 years.

Following the war, the sluggers returned. Some—Charlie Keller of the Yankees among them—found their home run stroke rusty, if not lost for good. That wasn't the case with Detroit's Hank Greenberg, who rejoined the Tigers midway through the 1945 season, in time to hit .311 with 13 homers and 60 RBI as he led the club to the AL pennant and a 4–3 World Series victory over the Cubs. But the following season, 1946, Greenberg established a precedent that doomsayers all the way back to Babe Ruth's Polo Grounds days had predicted. In leading the league with 44 home runs and 127 RBI, Greenberg managed only a .277 average, making him the first player ever to hit 40 or

Josh Gibson
An Uncrowned King

An 18-year-old boy—shy, muscular, and in only his second month as a pro ballplayer—stepped into the batter's box at Yankee Stadium and tapped the plate. Taking a vicious cut at a fastball, he sent it high over left field, past the spot where the legendary Jimmie Foxx had once blasted a Lefty Gomez pitch into third deck.

"It went over the roof . . . it went over everything!" claimed William "Judy" Johnson, spotting it from the home team dugout behind third base. Others who had a better view say the ball glanced off the back wall of the grandstand, falling back into the bullpen, but it hardly matters. Another foot or so and it would have cleared the roof and sailed out of the park, about as far as a ball can go in The House That Ruth Built.

The kid who hit it was strong, talented and black. His name was Josh Gibson. And he never made it to the major leagues.

Gibson did go on to set other long distance records in big league parks like Pittsburgh's Forbes Field and Cleveland's Municipal Stadium. In 1944 he drove six home runs into the faraway bleachers of Griffith Stadium in Washington, D.C. — and that was six more than all the right handers in the American League did that year.

Josh Gibson made his mark in 1936 as Satchel Paige's catcher on the Pittsburgh Crawfords, the classiest battery on what many say was the best Negro League team ever. His .385 lifetime batting average still stands as the highest in the black professional circuit. In 16 postseason games, at a time when blacks and whites played together only in exhibition, he hit .424 against major league pitchers. After he socked a home run off Dizzy Dean in 1934, Diz trotted over to the dugout, mopped his brow, and panted, "Josh, if you and Satch played with me and Paul on the Cardinals, we'd win the pennant by July Fourth and go fishin' the rest of the season."

Batting ahead of Buck Leonard on the Washington Homestead Grays, Gibson led the club to nine straight pennants between 1937 and 1945. Leonard and Gibson were unquestionably the most devastating home run duo in league ball between the era of Ruth and Gehrig and that of Mantle and Maris. Gibson and Leonard were so good that in 1942 Senators owner Clark Griffith talked to them about moving over to Washington's major league team, but he never followed up. If he had, the Senators might well have given the Yankees a run for their money as a baseball dynasty.

By the end of World War II it was clearly only a matter of time before black players would be integrated into the majors. Josh Gibson, undisputed king of the black sluggers, figured he would be the first to break the barrier. So did a lot of savvy sports

Josh Gibson (right), as near perfect a player as the game has ever seen, tempted major league owners but was never offered a contract. Before Gibson's rise to fame, Mule Suttles (far right) was often called "the Negro Babe Ruth."

fans. But in 1946 an unknown rookie, a kid from UCLA named Jackie Robinson, signed onto the Dodgers' Montreal farm team and soon made baseball history. That winter Josh Gibson was dead at 35, allegedly from a drug overdose. "They say Josh died of a brain hemorrhage," his friend outfielder Ted Paige recalls. "I say he died of a broken heart."

Josh Gibson was probably the best-known, but far from the only, black professional player for whom integration came too late. Most pioneers from the Negro Leagues' rough and ready barnstorming days had long since retired—Oscar Charleston, the Willie Mays of his day; Pop Lloyd, called "the black Honus Wagner"; Smokey Joe Williams, who outpolled Satchel Paige in a vote of experts to name the greatest black pitcher; Norman "Turkey" Stearnes, the all-time Negro League home run hitter, with 33 more than Gibson himself.

Many of the prewar black stars were simply too old to be considered when the doors swung open—players like James "Cool Papa" Bell who owned the Grays' center field and was reputedly the fastest man ever to wear spikes. He could score from first

on a single and proved it against Cleveland pitcher Bob Lemon and Red Sox catcher Ray Pardee in a 1947 postseason game—when Bell was 47 years old. In 46 games against white pitching, Cool Papa hit a warm .395.

Shortstop Willie Wells, often compared with Lou Boudreau, led the league in 1930 with a .404 average. His lifetime .358 batting pace and 111 home runs rank sixth in the Negro National League. Wells' style of play stunned Hall of Famers Charlie Gehringer, Heinie Manush and Harry Heilmann in a 1929 exhibition series. In the first game, Wells' ninth-inning triple knocked home the tying run, and he scored the winner a few moments later, kicking the ball out of catcher Wally Schang's hand. The next day he punched a pair of triples and stole home again. In the final game, he smashed three more hits, the last one bringing in the winning run, as the black team took the series three out of four.

Kiner's Big Seven

In his 10-year major league career, Ralph Kiner hit 369 home runs, an average of nearly 37 homers a season. But from1946 through 1952, Kiner averaged 42 homers and led or tied all National League sluggers in each of his first seven seasons. No one—not Babe Ruth, not Hank Aaron—began his career with such auspicious power.

The Top Five National League Home Run Leaders, 1946-1952

1946 Ralph Kiner 23
Johnny Mize 22, Enos Slaughter 18, Del Ennis 17, Stan Musial and Ron Northey 16

1947 Ralph Kiner and Johnny Mize tied at 51
Willard Marshall 36, Walker Cooper 35, Bobby Thomson 29

1948 Ralph Kiner and Johnny Mize tied at 40
Stan Musial 39, Hank Sauer 35, Del Ennis and Sid Gordon 30

1949 Ralph Kiner 54
Stan Musial 36, Hank Sauer 31, Bobby Thomson 27, Sid Gordon 26

1950 Ralph Kiner 47
Andy Pafko 36, Gil Hodges and Hank Sauer 32, Roy Campanella and Duke Snider 31

1951 Ralph Kiner 42
Gil Hodges 40, Roy Campanella 33, Stan Musial and Bobby Thomson 32

1952 Ralph Kiner and Hank Sauer tied at 37
Gil Hodges 32, Sid Gordon 25, Eddie Mathews 25

more homers in a season with a batting average less than .300. The great divide between hitting and slugging had begun.

On January 20, 1947, Josh Gibson died. He was 35. The most legendary slugger in the history of the Negro leagues went to his grave never having tested his power at the big league level. Three months after Gibson's death, Jackie Robinson broke in with the Brooklyn Dodgers, the first black player in the history of the majors.

The black sluggers who followed Jackie Robinson into the majors in the late 1940s profoundly influenced the nature of the power game during the decade to come. Larry Doby of the Indians, Hank Thompson of the Giants, and Roy Campanella and Jackie Robinson of the Dodgers were the only black sluggers on major league rosters by the end of the 1949 season. Three years later Doby and Luke Easter became the most feared home run tandem in the American League. By the end of the 1956 season, Willie Mays had already hit 51 homers in a year, Hank Aaron had won the National League home run crown with 44 round trippers, Ernie Banks had topped the 40-mark twice, and Frank Robinson had just completed a Rookie-of-the-Year season with 38 homers, 83 RBI, and a .290 average. Within ten years of Jackie Robinson's debut, three of the four top home run hitters of all time—Aaron, Mays, and Robinson—were playing in the majors. All were black, and all were cut in the best tradition of the complete slugger: they excelled at all aspects of the game.

In addition to Aaron, Mays, Robinson, and Banks, there were the two premier sluggers—Williams and Musial—from the preceding two decades, as well as Campanella, Yogi Berra, Gil Hodges, Vern Stephens, and the incom-

Cleveland center fielder Larry Doby became the first black player to win a home run title in 1952 when he led the American League with 32 homers. Six years earlier he had led the Newark Eagles to a Negro League World Series championship.

Ralph Kiner's explosive swing delivered 51 homers for Pittsburgh in 1947—including a record eight in four consecutive games.

parable Ralph Kiner, who led the National League in home runs during his first seven seasons.

But what truly distinguished the 1950s was the predominance of home run hitters. Never before had so many sluggers dominated so many positions. More than ever, outfielders outdistanced the field, particularly in center, where the three teams in the city of New York boasted three of the greatest ever, namely Mays, Mantle, and Snider—Willie, Mickey, and the Duke.

On any given day during the season, a New Yorker could take in a game at the Polo Grounds, Ebbets Field, or Yankee Stadium and watch one of three future Hall of Fame center fielders. Who was Number One depended on which fan you asked, and among Dodger, Giant, and Yankee rooters, objectivity was rare. Each was remarkable, and each played under tremendous expectations to excel, which they did. In addition to speed and exceptional fielding ability, Snider, Mays, and Mantle posted some incredible slugging numbers. From 1951 until the Dodgers and Giants moved west in 1957, the three center fielders combined for a .324 batting mark and averaged 107 RBI and 36 homers per season.

But Mays, Mantle, and Snider did not represent the growing trend of sluggers in the 1950s. Increasingly, more and more longball hitters were hitting just that—the long ball, and only the long ball. Strikeouts climbed, as did the number of homers. But at the same time, the serious singles hitter was beginning a comeback.

For example, in 1958, of the top five home run hitters in the American League, which Mickey Mantle led with 42, only Mantle, Rocky Colavito, and Bob Cerv hit .300 or better. On the other hand, of the top five batting leaders—including Pete Runnels, Harvey Kuenn, Al Kaline, and Vic Power—only Ted Williams,

Bobby Thomson's Shot

On August 11, 1951, the New York Giants were mired in last place, 13½ games behind the league-leading Brooklyn Dodgers. But the Giants—led by Bobby Thomson, Monte Irvin, rookie center fielder Willie Mays, and 23-game winners Sal Maglie and Larry Jansen—won 37 of their last 44 games to tie Brooklyn and force a three-game playoff.

Thomson's two-run homer won the first game for the Giants, but Dodger Clem Labine shut New York out in Game 2. Game 3 had Maglie and Don Newcombe clash in a pitcher's duel. Jackie Robinson's single scored Brooklyn shortstop Pee Wee Reese in the first, but the Giants tied it at 1–1 in the seventh on Thomson's sacrifice fly. In the eighth a wild pitch and singles by Andy Pafko and Billy Cox gave the Dodgers a 4–1 lead and an apparent lock on the pennant they should have clinched weeks before.

Reporters started toward the Dodger dugout and were told to pick up their passes for the next day's World Series game. They hadn't heard Newcombe complain to Jackie Robinson after the seventh that he was tired. "Get out there and pitch," Robinson said.

Alvin Dark led off the bottom of the ninth with a single off the glove of first baseman Gil Hodges. Despite the three-run lead, Hodges held Dark on, giving Don Mueller enough of a hole to poke a single into right field, sending Dark to third and 30,000 Giant fans into a frenzy. In the Dodger bullpen, Ralph Branca and Carl Erskine started warming up. Newcombe got Irvin on a pop fly to Hodges. Whitey Lockman then laced a line drive over Cox's head at third for a double, scoring Dark and sending Mueller to third. For Dodger skipper Charley Dressen, it was decision time. Newcombe was through, and not only had Branca pitched two days earlier

and given up a homer to Thomson that day, but he had already been beaten five times by the Giants that season. But bullpen coach Clyde Sukeforth said Erskine "didn't have anything," and that Branca was "really firing." Preacher Roe, 20–3 for Brooklyn that season, was being saved for Game 1 of the World Series, and Clem Labine had pitched nine innings the day before. So it was Branca.

Dressen could have walked Thomson, who had 31 homers and had battered the Dodgers all season, but that would have put the winning run on first. Branca started Thomson off with a fastball down the middle, and Thomson took it for strike one. Branca then wanted to waste a fastball up and in to set Thomson up for a curve away, but he got too much of the plate—and Bobby got too much of the ball. Thomson's liner to left center would have been caught in many parks, but it cleared the Polo Grounds' 315-foot sign, and pandemonium reigned.

While Thomson circled the bases, fans and players stormed the field, Branca walked off the mound, and Robinson stood stubbornly on the infield, making sure Thomson touched every base. While 15 million people watched the heroism on television, 80 million listening to the game on WMCA heard radio announcer Russ Hodges' now famous chant, "The Giants win the pennant!"

Sportswriter Red Smith proclaimed "The art of fiction is dead. Only the utterly impossible, the inexpressibly fantastic can ever be plausible again."

The Giants lost the World Series in six games to the Yankees. Branca fell off a chair and injured his pelvis during spring training the next year and won just twelve games in the next three seasons, and Thomson was traded to Milwaukee in 1954. But they will forever be frozen in time. Erskine had the right perspective. "That's the first time I've ever seen a big fat wallet flying into the grandstand."

Roger Maris was a low-average slugger but with a difference—he didn't strike out much. In 1961, when he hit 61 home runs to break Babe Ruth's record, he struck out just 67 times.

Power by Position

Prior to World War II the primary source of power was among outfielders, but by the 1950s there were sluggers at almost every position.

Most Home Runs

National League	Season			1950-1959	
Catcher	Roy Campanella	41, 1953		Roy Campanella	211
First Base	Ted Kluszewski	49, 1954		Gil Hodges	310
Second Base	Charley Neal	22, 1958		Red Schoendienst	69
Third Base	Eddie Mathews	47, 1953		Eddie Mathews	299
Shortstop	Ernie Banks	47, 1958		Ernie Banks	228
Left Field	Ralph Kiner	47, 1950		Ralph Kiner	201
Center Field	Willie Mays	51, 1955		Duke Snider	326
Right Field	Hank Aaron	44, 1957		Hank Aaron	179

American League	Season			1950-1959	
Catcher	Yogi Berra	30, 1952, '56		Yogi Berra	256
	Gus Triandos	30, 1958			
First Base	Walt Dropo	34, 1950		Eddie Robinson	121
Second Base	Bobby Doerr	27, 1950		Bobby Avila	80
Third Base	Al Rosen	43, 1953		Al Rosen	192
Shortstop	Vern Stephens	30, 1950		Eddie Joost	69
Left Field	Gus Zernial	42, 1953		Ted Williams	227
	Roy Sievers	42, 1957			
Center Field	Mickey Mantle	52, 1956		Mickey Mantle	280
Right Field	Rocky Colavito	42, 1959		Jackie Jensen	186

who led the league with a .328 mark, hit more than 16 home runs. Although the situation was not nearly so drastic in the National League where there was greater homer/average parity, there were still hints of the precedent set by Greenberg in 1946: Frank Thomas, whose 35 homers were second to Banks' 47, hit .281, while batting leader Richie Ashburn of the Phillies—he hit .350—managed just two round trippers.

By 1959, a popular argument among baseball fans revolved around who was more valuable to a team, the slugger or the hitter. The two talents were becoming that distinct. On April 17, 1960, the Cleveland Indians and Detroit Tigers pulled off a blockbuster trade. The Indians swapped Rocky Colavito straight up to the Tigers for Harvey Kuenn. In 1959, Colavito had tied with Harmon Killebrew for the league lead in homers with 42 and managed a paltry .257 batting average. Kuenn had led the league with a .353 average but hit only nine home runs. The Indians were clearly opting for on-base consistency as a winning strategy, while the Tigers added another powerful bat to an already strong lineup.

Which team made the best move? The 1961 Tigers won 101 games with Colavito in the lineup but finished second to Maris, Mantle, and the Yankees. Kuenn lasted a year with the fifth-place Indians, batted a mediocre .308, then went on to the pennant-winning San Francisco Giants in 1962.

The Colavito-Kuenn trade acknowledged the strategic role of the specialized hitter. Sluggers took their cue and dominated the decade, beginning in 1961 with Roger Maris' record 61 home runs, which he accompanied with an undistinguished .269 average. As a phenomenon of the times, specialization probably had more to do with strategy and managers'

6'1" 190 lbs.
BL TR
b 10/13/31

EDDIE MATHEWS
Third Base

Before Mike Schmidt there was Eddie Mathews, the king of homer-hitting third basemen. In the 1950s, it was Mathews—not Aaron, nor Mays, nor Mantle—who posed the greatest threat to Babe Ruth's career home run record.

Mathews broke in with the Braves in 1952 and hit 25 homers in the team's last year in Boston. The following year he led the NL with 47 home runs, drove in 135 runs, and hit .302. Mathews continued his 40-homer-a-year pace through 1955. By 1957, when the Braves won their first pennant in Milwaukee and beat the Yankees in the World Series, Mathews had hit 222 home runs and he was still just 26 years old.

By 1962, after ten years in the majors, Mathews was averaging 37 home runs a season, a pace that exceeded Ruth's by 100 homers and Aaron's by 15. In addition, his nine consecutive seasons of 30 or more homers established a National League record. Although he couldn't sustain the promise of those first ten years, Mathews completed his 17-year career with 512 lifetime homers, twelfth on the all-time list.

Mathews was hurt by playing most of his career in Milwaukee's County Stadium, where he hit just 46 percent of his lifetime home runs, the lowest figure of any player with 500 or more home runs. Ironically, Mathews was the manager of the Atlanta Braves when Hank Aaron broke Babe Ruth's 714 career home run record in 1974.

Willie Mays

How great was Willie Mays? He was great enough to make everyone around him play better. He was great enough to make Leo Durocher seem kindly.

Durocher, Mays' first manager with the New York Giants, the man known for saying that "nice guys finish last," was the man who knew Willie Mays best. He described Mays this way: "If somebody came up and hit .450, stole 100 bases, and performed a miracle on the field every day, I'd still look you in the eye and say Willie was better. He could do the five things you have to do to be a superstar: hit, hit with power, run, throw, and field. And he had that other ingredient. He lit up the room when he came in. He was a joy to be around."

But in May 1951, Willie Mays was asking Durocher to send him back to the minors. A skinny, emotional 20-year-old, Mays had gone 0 for his first 12 major league at-bats after being called up from Minneapolis where he'd batted .477. But Durocher would have none of it. "You're my center fielder from now until the end of the season. Now forget about everything else. Just go out and play baseball," Durocher told his flustered rookie. Then he penciled Mays into the lineup to face Milwaukee's Warren Spahn, the league's best left hander.

On his next trip to the plate, Mays timed Spahn's 1–1 curveball perfectly and hit it over the left field roof at the Polo Grounds. "I'll never forgive myself," Spahn said years later. "We might have gotten rid of Willie [forever] if only I'd struck him out."

That single home run was the beginning of a magical season and a magical career. With it, Mays found his confidence and his teammates rallied behind him, as the Giants came from $13\frac{1}{2}$ games back to win the National League pennant on Bobby Thomson's ninth-inning playoff homer against the Brooklyn Dodgers. Mays won the Rookie of the Year award on the strength of 20 homers, 68 RBI, and a .274 batting average.

But there was more to Mays than the numbers. Anyone who saw him play that rookie season knew immediately that Mays was one of the game's truly gifted players, one who could beat you at the plate, in the field, on the bases, and in other ways as well. Mays had a vibrant personality and an infectious, childlike love for the game.

In his 22-year career, Mays piled up numbers that earned him a spot among baseball's true elite. One of the game's most aggressive hitters, he ranks third all-time in homers with 660 and in total bases with 6,066. He ranks fourth in extra base hits with 1,323, fifth in runs scored with 2,062, and seventh in RBI with 1,903. He led the National League in home runs and stolen bases four times each and was the first player ever to hit 50 homers and steal 20 bases in a season. Mays led the league in slugging average five times, triples three times, and runs scored twice. And in 1954 he won the NL batting title with a .345 mark.

In center field, Mays seemed superhuman. Quite simply, he was the greatest outfielder who ever played. Mays has more putouts—7,095—than any outfielder in history. He loved to play shallow, and in his first six years as a Giant this meant an even greater challenge, as Mays roamed the most spacious cen-

In 1961 Mays (above) hit 40 home runs, starting a six-year power streak in which he averaged 44 homers a season. Mays (left), as much a leader off the field as on, became the Giants' team captain in 1964 under manager and former teammate Alvin Dark.

Mays (above) played in his fourth and last World Series in 1973 with the New York Mets. With San Francisco (below), Mays inspired such young stars as Willie McCovey, Orlando Cepeda, and Juan Marichal.

ter field in baseball. The center field fence at the Polo Grounds was 483 feet away from home plate. In Game 1 of the 1954 World Series, Mays traveled to the 450-foot mark to make what became known simply as "The Catch," robbing Cleveland's Vic Wertz of a game-winning hit with an over-the-shoulder grab. Mays came in on the ball pretty well, too. Former Giant and Cardinal first baseman Bill White swears he saw Mays catch a ball in the infield. "The second baseman misjudged the ball, and Willie caught it between first and second," White said.

His arm was as strong and as accurate as that of anyone who ever played the outfield. During a game with the Dodgers in 1951, Mays, who had been playing the right-handed Carl Furillo to pull, streaked across the outfield to spear Furillo's 400-foot drive on the dead run. Without stopping, Mays spun and threw a strike in the air to home plate to cut down Billy Cox, who had tagged up at third.

Perhaps Mays' greatest achievement was that he captured the hearts of New York's demanding fans. But like everything else he did, Mays made that, too, look easy. Kids loved him. Born and raised in Westfield, Alabama, Mays could be found on his off days playing stick ball with kids on the streets of Harlem.

Mays' career was interrupted by military service in 1952 and 1953. In 1954 he returned to lead the Giants to a World Series sweep of the Cleveland Indians, winning Most Valuable Player honors for his .345 batting average, 41 homers, and 110 RBI. That year he was also named to his first All-Star team, the first of his 20 straight All-Star selections.

The Giants moved to San Francisco in 1958, and Mays continued his spectacular play. From 1958 to 1968, the Giants never dropped below fifth place in the National League, winning one pennant and finishing second four times. Mays averaged 36 homers and 104 RBI during that period, and hit over .300 seven times.

In 1962, the expansion of the National League brought Mays and the San Francisco Giants back to

WILLIE MAYS

Outfield
New York Giants 1951-1957
San Francisco Giants 1958-1971
New York Mets 1972-1973
Hall of Fame 1979

GAMES *(6th all time)*	**2,992**
AT BATS *(6th all time)*	**10,881**
BATTING AVERAGE	
Career	**.302**
Season High	**.347**
BATTING TITLES	**1954**
SLUGGING AVERAGE	
Career *(10th all time)*	**.557**
Season High	**.667**
HITS	
Career *(9th all time)*	**3,283**
Season High	**208**
DOUBLES	
Career	**523**
Season High	**43**
TRIPLES	
Career	**140**
Season High	**20**
HOME RUNS	
Career *(3rd all time)*	**660**
Season High	**52**
TOTAL BASES *(3rd all time)*	**6,066**
EXTRA BASE HITS *(4th all time)*	**1,323**
RUNS BATTED IN	
Career *(7th all time)*	**1,903**
Season High	**141**
RUNS	
Career *(5th all time)*	**2,062**
Season High	**130**
WORLD SERIES	**1951, 1954**
	1962, 1973
MOST VALUABLE PLAYER	
	1954, 1965

the Polo Grounds. In his first game against the New York Mets in his old haunts, Mays homered, inspiring Arthur Daley of *The New York Times* to write: "The center field turf at the Polo Grounds looks normal this weekend for the first time in five years. Willie Mays has come home." That year also brought another wild Giant-Dodger pennant race, this one on a different coast. Mays' homer on the last day of the season gave the Giants a 2–1 win over Houston and forced another three-game playoff for the pennant. Mays homered twice in an 8–0 Giant win in the first game, then keyed a four-run rally in the ninth inning of the third game, as the Giants snatched another pennant away from the Dodgers.

In 1964 Mays became baseball's first black team captain and responded with 47 homers that year and 52 the next. Only Mays and Ralph Kiner have had two 50-homer seasons in the National League. His production dropped off somewhat after 1966, though he did hit 28 homers in 1970 and led the league in walks in 1971. In 1972, at the age of 41, Mays was traded to the Mets, where he closed out his remarkable career in 1973.

With his combination of speed and power, Mays led the NL in triples in three of his six years with the New York Giants.

Best of the bulky sluggers of the 1960s, Minnesota's Harmon Killebrew (center right) has the second lowest batting average —.256—among the top 20 all-time home run hitters. His power led the Twins to division titles in 1969 and 1970.

Third baseman Ron Santo provided more than just offense for the Cubs—he won five straight Gold Glove awards from 1964 to 1968.

changing perception of the game than with players' abilities. Norm Cash's league-leading .361 average in 1961 was gravy to his 41 homers, the meat and potatoes of Detroit manager Bob Scheffing's season.

In fact, many home run hitters still hit for a decent average. In 1961, when an unprecedented eight players—Maris, Mantle, Cash, Colavito, Mays, Orlando Cepeda, Jim Gentile, and Harmon Killebrew—hit 40 or more home runs, all but Maris, Colavito, and Killebrew hit better than .300, and the latter two hit .290 and .288, respectively. While the durable sluggers of the 1950s—Aaron, Mathews, Mays, Robinson, Mantle, Colavito, Kaline, and Ken Boyer—kept homering away—Williams retired in 1960, Musial in 1963—a new breed emerged. Among them were Cepeda, Willie McCovey, Billy Williams, Willie Stargell, Ron Santo, Leon Wagner, Carl Yastrzemski, Boog Powell, Frank Howard, and Reggie Jackson. Most of these sluggers earned their keep by way of the long ball, but none did it so profitably as Harmon Killebrew of the Twins. From 1960 to 1969 Killebrew averaged 39 home runs a season. He ended his career with 573 homers, the most by any right-handed hitter in American League history. He never once hit higher than .288.

In 1969, at the age of 33, Killebrew posted career highs with 49 home runs and 140 RBI and led the AL in both departments. Finishing third behind Killebrew—with 47 homers and 118 RBI—was an Oakland Athletics outfielder ten years Killebrew's junior: Reginald Martinez Jackson. Earlier that year, Jackson, with only one full season behind him, was on a pace to break Maris' single-season home run record. By the All-Star Game, he had already hit 37 home runs but managed only ten during the second half of the season. Jackson became Killebrew's successor, the prototypical all-or-nothing swinger. He led the league in strikeouts each of his first four full seasons and ended his

Placed at the heart of one of the most potent lineups ever, Cincinnati catcher Johnny Bench drove in 1,013 runs, more than any other player in the 1970s.

Outfielder Billy Williams led some of the best and most power-laden teams never to win a pennant—the Chicago Cubs of the 1960s and early 1970s. The Cubs' experience called into question the theory that, in baseball, power prevails.

career with a record 2,597 strikeouts—almost 1,000 more than Killebrew and twice as many as Babe Ruth. But Jackson's 563 career homers went a long way in making his team a winner—he played in eleven league championship series and five World Series.

All the glory that came from Jackson's go-for-broke stroke eluded Dave Kingman, who could hit a ball as far and as hard as anyone, and just as often. In 16 seasons he slugged 442 home runs, but he also batted just .236 and couldn't field. Kingman was living proof that the home run was not a cure-all. His only postseason appearance came in 1971, his rookie season with the Giants. Thereafter, as often as he homered—and he led the National League twice—his homers did not translate as victories. No fewer than seven teams bought Kingman's services—in 1977 he actually played for the Mets, the Padres, the Angels, and the Yankees. His calling card was "Have Bat Will Travel"; he was the designated home run hitter of the 1970s.

To be fair to Kingman, consider the times. In 1973, the American League club owners, in the role of Dr. Frankenstein, invented the monster known as the designated hitter. The following year, Henry Aaron hit his 715th career home run to break Babe Ruth's all-time record and was just a year away from being reduced to DH status himself. Baseball, and the American League in particular, had turned homer happy. It was as if the sport did not know what to do with itself. Even the players looked desperate in their polyester, multi-colored double-knits. Zippers replaced buttons. Expando waistbands knocked belts for a loop. Every trend was catered to.

Such was the case of the home run and the role of the slugger. Owners, it seemed, viewed the game with a kind of tunnel vision that isolated the home run and the slugger. Pittsburgh's Willie Stargell averaged 30 homers from

In 1977 Cincinnati right fielder George Foster's slugging surpassed not only his Big Red Machine teammates, but the entire National League. His 52 homers in 1977 have not been equaled since.

In 1988, Montreal first baseman Andres Galarraga blossomed into a premier slugger and became a member of the National League's new group of multitalented big men. At 6'3", 235 lbs., Galarraga is considered by many to be one of the best-fielding first baseman of all time.

1970 to 1979, while Boston's Jim Rice averaged 34 in his first five full seasons. With such emphasis on individuals, it's hardly surprising that the players who dominated the decade were with teams that emphasized playing unselfishly, as a unit. The Cincinnati Reds, with Johnny Bench, Tony Perez, George Foster, and Joe Morgan, led the home run parade. But despite expansion, the 162-game schedule, and the American League's wishful thinking, the total home run production in the major leagues fell off dramatically in the 1970s.

By 1980, two sluggers were about to come of age. That season, Dale Murphy of the Braves and Eddie Murray of the Orioles reached the 30-homer plateau for the first time in their careers. But they also proved that their total game was not limited to the home run. The following season, Dave Winfield signed as a free agent with the Yankees. An excellent athlete who had been drafted in basketball and football as well as in baseball out of the University of Minnesota in 1969, Winfield saw his career—and competitive edge—foundering after eight years with the San Diego Padres. New York became the stage where he could showcase his total game. In his first eight seasons with the Yankees, Winfield twice hit .320 or higher, twice hit 32 or more homers, and drove in 100 or more runs six times. By the end of the decade he had become a kind of model: the *total* player.

In Winfield's wake came such sluggers as Jose Canseco, Kirby Puckett, Don Mattingly, Eric Davis, and Kevin McReynolds. And not a one looked or played anything like the Babe, though in each a fan could see a touch of at least one of the many sluggers who in 60 years had ensured that the power game would live forever. ◗▮

Cincinnati left fielder Eric Davis is the fastest of the new-age sluggers. In 1987 Davis came within three homers of beating Oakland's Jose Canseco to the first 40–40 season, hitting 37 homers and stealing 50 bases.

All-Time Slugging Leaders

All records are accurate through the 1989 baseball season.

Hits

Career		Season		
1. Pete Rose	4,256	1. George Sisler	1920	257
2. Ty Cobb	4,191	2. Lefty O'Doul	1929	254
3. Hank Aaron	3,771	– Bill Terry	1930	254
4. Stan Musial	3,630	4. Al Simmons	1925	253
5. Tris Speaker	3,515	5. Rogers Hornsby	1922	250
6. Honus Wagner	3,430	– Chuck Klein	1930	250
7. Carl Yastrzemski	3,419	7. Ty Cobb	1911	248
8. Eddie Collins	3,311	8. George Sisler	1922	246
9. Willie Mays	3,283	9. Willie Keeler	1897	243
10. Napoleon Lajoie	3,251	10. H. Manush, Ba. Herman		241

Walks

Career		Season		
1. Babe Ruth	2,056	1. Babe Ruth	1923	170
2. Ted Williams	2,019	2. Ted Williams	1947	162
3. Joe Morgan	1,865	– Ted Williams	1949	162
4. Carl Yastrzemski	1,845	4. Ted Williams	1946	156
5. Mickey Mantle	1,734	5. Eddie Yost	1956	151
6. Mel Ott	1,708	6. Eddie Joost	1949	149
7. Eddie Yost	1,614	7. Babe Ruth	1920	148
8. Stan Musial	1,599	– Eddie Stanky	1945	148
9. Pete Rose	1,566	– Jimmy Wynn	1969	148
10. H. Killebrew	1,559	10. Jimmy Sheckard	1911	147

Doubles

Career		Season		
1. Tris Speaker	793	1. Earl Webb	1931	67
2. Pete Rose	746	2. George Burns	1926	64
3. Stan Musial	725	– Joe Medwick	1936	64
4. Ty Cobb	724	4. Hank Greenberg	1934	63
5. Honus Wagner	651	5. Paul Waner	1932	62
6. Napoleon Lajoie	648	6. Charlie Gehringer	1936	60
7. Carl Yastrzemski	646	7. Tris Speaker	1923	59
8. Hank Aaron	624	– Chuck Klein	1930	59
9. Paul Waner	603	9. Billy Herman	1935	57
10. Charlie Gehringer	574	– Billy Herman	1936	57

Triples

Career		Season		
1. Sam Crawford	312	1. Owen Wilson	1912	36
2. Ty Cobb	297	2. Dave Orr	1886	31
3. Honus Wagner	252	– Heinie Reitz	1894	31
4. Jake Beckley	244	4. Perry Werden	1893	29
5. Roger Connor	233	5. Harry Davis	1897	28
6. Fred Clarke	223	6. George Davis	1893	27
– Tris Speaker	223	– Sam Thompson	1894	27
8. Dan Brouthers	206	– Jimmy Williams	1899	27
9. Joe Kelley	194	9. Five players tied		26
10. Paul Waner	190			

Home Runs

Career		Season		
1. Hank Aaron	755	1. Roger Maris	1961	61
2. Babe Ruth	714	2. Babe Ruth	1927	60
3. Willie Mays	660	3. Babe Ruth	1921	59
4. Frank Robinson	586	4. Jimmie Foxx	1932	58
5. Harmon Killebrew	573	– Hank Greenberg	1938	58
6. Reggie Jackson	563	6. Hack Wilson	1930	56
7. Mike Schmidt	548	7. Babe Ruth	1920	54
8. Mickey Mantle	536	– Babe Ruth	1928	54
9. Jimmie Foxx	534	– Ralph Kiner	1949	54
10. W. McCovey, T. Williams	521	– Mickey Mantle	1961	54

Extra-Base Hits

Career		Season		
1. Hank Aaron	1,477	1. Babe Ruth	1921	119
2. Stan Musial	1,377	2. Lou Gehrig	1927	117
3. Babe Ruth	1,356	3. Chuck Klein	1930	107
4. Willie Mays	1,323	4. Chuck Klein	1932	103
5. Lou Gehrig	1,190	– Hank Greenberg	1937	103
6. Frank Robinson	1,186	– Stan Musial	1948	103
7. Carl Yastrzemski	1,157	7. Rogers Hornsby	1922	102
8. Ty Cobb	1,139	8. Lou Gehrig	1930	100
9. Tris Speaker	1,133	– Jimmie Foxx	1932	100
10. T. Williams, J. Foxx	1,117	10. B. Ruth, H. Greenberg		99

Runs

Career		Season		
1. Ty Cobb	2,245	1. Billy Hamilton	1894	196
2. Babe Ruth	2,174	2. Tom Brown	1891	177
– Hank Aaron	2,174	– Babe Ruth	1921	177
4. Pete Rose	2,165	4. Tip O' Neill	1887	167
5. Willie Mays	2,062	– Joe Kelley	1894	167
6. Stan Musial	1,949	– Lou Gehrig	1936	167
7. Lou Gehrig	1,888	7. Billy Hamilton	1895	166
8. Tris Speaker	1,881	8. Willie Keeler	1894	165
9. Mel Ott	1,859	9. A. Latham, B. Ruth, L. Gehrig		163
10. Frank Robinson	1,829			

RBI

Career		Season		
1. Hank Aaron	2,297	1. Hack Wilson	1930	190
2. Babe Ruth	2,211	2. Lou Gehrig	1931	184
3. Lou Gehrig	1,990	3. Hank Greenberg	1937	183
4. Ty Cobb	1,961	4. Lou Gehrig	1927	175
5. Stan Musial	1,951	– Jimmie Foxx	1938	175
6. Jimmie Foxx	1,921	6. Lou Gehrig	1930	174
7. Willie Mays	1,903	7. Babe Ruth	1921	171
8. Mel Ott	1,860	8. Chuck Klein	1930	170
9. Carl Yastrzemski	1,844	– Hank Greenberg	1935	170
10. Ted Williams	1,839	10. Jimmie Foxx	1932	169

Batting Average

Career		Season		
1. Ty Cobb	.367	1. Hugh Duffy	1894	.438
2. Rogers Hornsby	.358	2. Tip O'Neill	1887	.435
3. Joe Jackson	.356	3. Willie Keeler	1897	.432
– Wade Boggs	.356	4. Ross Barnes	1876	.429
5. Ed Delahanty	.345	5. Rogers Hornsby	1924	.424
– Willie Keeler	.345	6. Jesse Burkett	1895	.423
7. Billy Hamilton	.344	7. Napoleon Lajoie	1901	.422
– Tris Speaker	.344	8. Ty Cobb	1911	.420
– Ted Williams	.344	– George Sisler	1922	.420
10. D. Brouthers, P. Browning	.343	10. Tuck Turner	1894	.416

Slugging Average

Career		Season		
1. Babe Ruth	.690	1. Babe Ruth	1920	.847
2. Ted Williams	.634	2. Babe Ruth	1921	.846
3. Lou Gehrig	.632	3. Babe Ruth	1927	.772
4. Jimmie Foxx	.609	4. Lou Gehrig	1927	.765
5. Hank Greenberg	.605	5. Babe Ruth	1923	.764
6. Joe DiMaggio	.579	6. Rogers Hornsby	1925	.756
7. Rogers Hornsby	.577	7. Jimmie Foxx	1932	.749
8. Johnny Mize	.562	8. Babe Ruth	1924	.739
9. Stan Musial	.559	9. Babe Ruth	1926	.737
10. W. Mays, M. Mantle	.557	10. Ted Williams	1941	.735

Batting Average, Home Run and Runs Batted In Champions, 1901-1989

National League

Year	BA		HR		RBI		Year	BA		HR		RBI	
1901	J. Burkett	.382	S. Crawford	16	H. Wagner	126	1943	S. Musial	.357	B. Nicholson	29	Nicholson	128
1902	G. Beaumont	.357	T. Leach	6	Wagner	91	1944	D. Walker	.357	Nicholson	33	Nicholson	122
1903	Wagner	.355	J. Sheckard	9	S. Mertes	104	1945	P. Cavarretta	.355	T. Holmes	28	D.Walker	124
1904	Wagner	.349	H. Lumley	9	B. Dahlen	80	1946	Musial	.365	R. Kiner	23	E. Slaughter	130
1905	C. Seymour	.377	F. Odwell	9	Seymour	121	1947	H. Walker	.363	Kiner, Mize	51	Mize	138
1906	Wagner	.339	T. Jordan	12	J. Nealon, H. Steinfeldt	83	1948	Musial	.376	Kiner, Mize	40	Musial	131
1907	Wagner	.350	D. Brain	10	S. Magee	85	1949	J. Robinson	.342	Kiner	54	Kiner	127
1908	Wagner	.354	Jordan	12	Wagner	109	1950	Musial	.346	Kiner	47	D. Ennis	126
1909	Wagner	.339	R. Murray	7	Wagner	100	1951	Musial	.355	Kiner	42	M. Irvin	121
1910	Magee	.331	F. Beck, W. Schulte	10	Magee	123	1952	Musial	.336	Kiner, H. Sauer	37	Sauer	121
1911	Wagner	.334	Schulte	21	Schulte	121	1953	C. Furillo	.344	E. Mathews	47	Campanella	142
1912	H. Zimmerman	.372	Zimmerman	14	Zimmerman	103	1954	W. Mays	.345	Kluszewski	49	Kluszewski	141
1913	J. Daubert	.350	G. Cravath	19	Cravath	128	1955	R. Ashburn	.338	Mays	51	D. Snider	136
1914	Daubert	.329	Cravath	19	Magee	103	1956	H. Aaron	.328	Snider	43	Musial	109
1915	L. Doyle	.320	Cravath	24	Cravath	115	1957	Musial	.351	Aaron	44	Aaron	132
1916	H. Chase	.339	D. Robertson, C. Williams	12	Zimmerman	83	1958	Ashburn	.350	E. Banks	47	Banks	129
1917	E. Roush	.341	Robertson, Cravath	12	Zimmerman	102	1959	Aaron	.355	Mathews	46	Banks	143
1918	Z. Wheat	.335	Cravath	8	Magee	76	1960	D. Groat	.325	Banks	41	Aaron	126
1919	Roush	.321	Cravath	12	H. Myers	73	1961	R. Clemente	.351	O. Cepeda	46	Cepeda	142
1920	R. Hornsby	.370	Williams	15	G. Kelly, Hornsby	94	1962	T. Davis	.346	Mays	49	Davis	153
1921	Hornsby	.397	Kelly	23	Hornsby	126	1963	Davis	.326	Aaron, W. McCovey	44	Aaron	130
1922	Hornsby	.401	Hornsby	42	Hornsby	152	1964	Clemente	.339	Mays	47	K. Boyer	119
1923	Hornsby	.384	C. Williams	41	I. Meusel	125	1965	Clemente	.329	Mays	52	D. Johnson	130
1924	Hornsby	.424	J. Fournier	27	Kelly	136	1966	M. Alou	.342	Aaron	44	Aaron	127
1925	Hornsby	.403	Hornsby	39	Hornsby	143	1967	Clemente	.357	Aaron	39	Cepeda	111
1926	B. Hargrave	.353	H. Wilson	21	J. Bottomley	120	1968	P. Rose	.335	McCovey	36	McCovey	105
1927	P. Waner	.380	Wilson, Williams	30	Waner	131	1969	Rose	.348	McCovey	45	McCovey	126
1928	Hornsby	.387	Wilson, Bottomley	31	Bottomley	136	1970	R. Carty	.366	J. Bench	45	Bench	148
1929	L. O'Doul	.398	C. Klein	43	Wilson	159	1971	J. Torre	.363	W. Stargell	48	Torre	137
1930	B. Terry	.401	Wilson	56	Wilson	190	1972	B. Williams	.333	Bench	40	Bench	125
1931	C. Hafey	.349	Klein	31	Klein	121	1973	Rose	.338	Stargell	44	Stargell	119
1932	O'Doul	.368	Klein, Ott	38	D. Hurst	143	1974	R. Garr	.353	M.Schmidt	36	Bench	129
1933	Klein	.368	Klein	28	Klein	120	1975	B. Madlock	.354	Schmidt	38	G. Luzinski	120
1934	Waner	.362	M. Ott, R. Collins	35	Ott	135	1976	Madlock	.339	Schmidt	38	G. Foster	121
1935	A. Vaughan	.385	W. Berger	34	Berger	130	1977	D. Parker	.338	Foster	52	Foster	149
1936	Waner	.373	Ott	33	J. Medwick	138	1978	Parker	.334	Foster	40	Foster	120
1937	Medwick	.374	Ott, Medwick	31	Medwick	154	1979	K. Hernandez	.344	D. Kingman	48	D. Winfield	118
1938	E. Lombardi	.342	Ott	36	Medwick	122	1980	B. Buckner	.324	Schmidt	48	Schmidt	121
1939	J. Mize	.349	Mize	28	McCormick	128	1981	Madlock	.341	Schmidt	31	Schmidt	91
1940	D. Garms	.355	Mize	43	Mize	137	1982	A. Oliver	.331	Kingman	37	D. Murphy, Oliver	109
1941	P. Reiser	.343	D. Camilli	34	Camilli	120	1983	Madlock	.323	Schmidt	40	Murphy	121
1942	Lombardi	.330	Ott	30	Mize	110	1984	T. Gwynn	.351	Murphy, Schmidt	36	G. Carter, Schmidt	106
							1985	W. McGee	.353	Murphy	37	Parker	125
							1986	T. Raines	.334	Schmidt	37	Schmidt	119
							1987	Gwynn	.370	A. Dawson	49	Dawson	137
							1988	Gwynn	.313	D. Strawberry	39	W. Clark	109
							1989	Gwynn	.336	K. Mitchell	47	K. Mitchell	125

Batting Average, Home Run and Runs Batted In Champions, 1901-1989

American League

Year	BA		HR		RBI	
1901	N. Lajoie	.422	Lajoie	13	Lajoie	125
1902	E. Delahanty	.376	S. Seybold	16	B. Freeman	121
1903	Lajoie	.355	Freeman	13	Freeman	104
1904	Lajoie	.381	H. Davis	10	Lajoie	102
1905	E. Flick	.306	Davis	8	Davis	83
1906	G. Stone	.358	Davis	12	Davis	96
1907	T. Cobb	.350	Davis	8	Cobb	116
1908	Cobb	.324	Crawford	7	Cobb	108
1909	Cobb	.377	Cobb	9	Cobb	107
1910	Cobb	.385	J. Stahl	10	Crawford	120
1911	Cobb	.420	F. Baker	11	Cobb	144
1912	Cobb	.410	T. Speaker, Baker	10	Baker	133
1913	Cobb	.390	Baker	12	Baker	126
1914	Cobb	.368	Baker	9	Crawford	104
1915	Cobb	.369	B. Roth	7	B. Veach, Crawford	112
1916	Speaker	.386	W. Pipp	12	D. Pratt	103
1917	Cobb	.383	Pipp	9	Veach	103
1918	Cobb	.382	B. Ruth, T. Walker	11	Veach	78
1919	Cobb	.384	Ruth	29	Ruth	114
1920	G. Sisler	.407	Ruth	54	Ruth	137
1921	H. Heilmann	.394	Ruth	59	Ruth	171
1922	Sisler	.420	K. Williams	39	Williams	155
1923	Heilmann	.403	Ruth	41	Ruth, Speaker	130
1924	Ruth	.378	Ruth	46	G. Goslin	129
1925	Heilmann	.393	B. Meusel	33	Meusel	138
1926	H. Manush	.378	Ruth	47	Ruth	145
1927	Heilmann	.398	Ruth	60	L. Gehrig	175
1928	Goslin	.379	Ruth	54	Ruth, Gehrig	142
1929	L. Fonseca	.369	Ruth	46	A. Simmons	157
1930	Simmons	.381	Ruth	49	Gehrig	174
1931	Simmons	.390	Ruth, Gehrig	46	Gehrig	184
1932	D. Alexander	.367	J. Foxx	58	Foxx	169
1933	Foxx	.356	Foxx	48	Foxx	163
1934	Gehrig	.363	Gehrig	49	Gehrig	165
1935	B. Myer	.349	Foxx, H. Greenberg	36	Greenberg	170
1936	L. Appling	.388	Gehrig	49	H. Trosky	162
1937	C. Gehringer	.371	J. DiMaggio	46	Greenberg	183
1938	Foxx	.349	Greenberg	58	Foxx	175
1939	DiMaggio	.381	Foxx	35	T. Williams	145
1940	DiMaggio	.352	Greenberg	41	Greenberg	150
1941	Williams	.406	Williams	37	DiMaggio	125
1942	Williams	.356	Williams	36	Williams	137
1943	Appling	.328	R. York	34	York	118
1944	L. Boudreau	.327	N. Etten	22	V. Stephens	109
1945	S. Stirnweiss	.309	Stephens	24	Etten	111
1946	M. Vernon	.353	Greenberg	44	Greenberg	127

Year	BA		HR		RBI	
1947	Williams	.343	Williams	32	Williams	114
1948	Williams	.369	DiMaggio	39	DiMaggio	155
1949	G. Kell	.343	Williams	43	Williams, Stephens	159
1950	B. Goodman	.354	A. Rosen	37	Stephens, W. Dropo	144
1951	F. Fain	.344	G. Zernial	33	Zernial	129
1952	Fain	.327	L. Doby	32	Rosen	105
1953	Vernon	.337	Rosen	43	Rosen	145
1954	B. Avila	.341	Doby	32	Doby	126
1955	A. Kaline	.340	M. Mantle	37	R. Boone, J. Jensen	116
1956	Mantle	.353	Mantle	52	Mantle	130
1957	Williams	.388	R. Sievers	42	Sievers	114
1958	Williams	.328	Mantle	42	Jensen	122
1959	H. Kuenn	.353	R. Colavito, H. Killebrew	42	Jensen	112
1960	P. Runnels	.320	Mantle	40	R. Maris	112
1961	N. Cash	.361	Maris	61	Maris	142
1962	Runnels	.326	Killebrew	48	Killebrew	126
1963	C. Yastrzemski	.321	Killebrew	45	D. Stuart	118
1964	T. Oliva	.323	Killebrew	49	B. Robinson	118
1965	Oliva	.321	T. Conigliaro	32	Colavito	108
1966	F. Robinson	.316	Robinson	49	Robinson	122
1967	Yastrzemski	.326	Yastrzemski, Killebrew	44	Yastrzemski	121
1968	Yastrzemski	.301	F. Howard	44	K. Harrelson	109
1969	R. Carew	.332	Killebrew	49	Killebrew	140
1970	A. Johnson	.329	Howard	44	Howard	126
1971	Oliva	.337	B. Melton	33	Killebrew	119
1972	Carew	.318	D. Allen	37	Allen	113
1973	Carew	.350	R. Jackson	32	Jackson	117
1974	Carew	.364	Allen	32	J. Burroughs	118
1975	Carew	.359	G. Scott, Jackson	36	Scott	109
1976	G. Brett	.333	G. Nettles	32	L. May	109
1977	Carew	.388	J. Rice	39	L. Hisle	119
1978	Carew	.333	Rice	46	Rice	139
1979	F. Lynn	.333	G. Thomas	45	D. Baylor	139
1980	Brett	.390	Jackson, B. Oglivie	41	C. Cooper	122
1981	C. Lansford	.336	E. Murray, B. Grich, T. Armas, Dw. Evans	22	Murray	78
1982	W. Wilson	.332	Jackson, Thomas	39	H. McRae	133
1983	W. Boggs	.361	Rice	39	Cooper, Rice	126
1984	D. Mattingly	.343	Armas	43	Armas	123
1985	Boggs	.368	Da. Evans	40	Mattingly	145
1986	Boggs	.357	J. Barfield	40	J. Carter	121
1987	Boggs	.363	M. McGwire	49	G. Bell	134
1988	Boggs	.366	J. Canseco	42	Canseco	124
1989	K. Puckett	.339	F. McGriff	36	R. Sierra	119

INDEX

FOR FURTHER READING

Craig Carter, *The Complete Baseball Record Book*. The Sporting News, 1988.

Robert Creamer, *Babe. The Legend Comes to Life*. Simon & Schuster, 1974.

Bill James, *The Bill James Historical Baseball Abstract*. Villard Books, 1988.

Charley Lau, *The Art of Hitting .300*. E.P. Dutton, 1986.

Philip J. Lowry, *Green Cathedrals*. Society for American Baseball Research, 1986.

David S. Neft and Richard M. Cohen, *The Sports Encyclopedia: Baseball*. St. Martin's Press, 1987.

Daniel Okrent and Harris Lewine, *The Ultimate Baseball Book*. Houghton Mifflin Company, 1981.

Joseph L. Reichler, *The Baseball Encyclopedia*. Macmillan Publishing Company, 1988.

Ted Williams and John Underwood, *The Science of Hitting*. Simon & Schuster, 1986.

PICTURE CREDITS

Front cover: Mickey Mantle by Marvin E. Newman.

Back cover: Andre Dawson by Jerry Wachter/*Sports Illustrated.*

A Great Day at the Plate
Pg. 4-5 Richard Hamilton Smith; 6 Tony Inzerillo; 7 Richard Hamilton Smith; 8 (left) David Walberg; 8 (right) Heinz Kluetmeier/*Sports Illustrated*; 9 David Walberg; 10 © 1979 The Philadelphia *Inquirer*, reprinted by permission; 11 (top left) Heinz Kluetmeier/*Sports Illustrated*; 11 (bottom right) Nancy Hogue; 12 Richard Hamilton Smith; 13 (left) David Walberg; 13 (right) Richard Hamilton Smith.

The Stick and the Ball
Pg. 14-15 Walter Iooss Jr./*Sports Illustrated*; 16 (top) Brown Brothers; 16 (bottom) AP/Wide World Photos; 17 AP/Wide World Photos; 18 (top) UPI/Bettmann Newsphotos; 18 (bottom) National Baseball Library, Cooperstown, New York; 19 National Baseball Library, Cooperstown, New York; 20 (left) Joel Zwink/ALLSPORT USA; 20 (right) Adrian Murrell/ALLSPORT USA; 21 Geoffrey C. Clifford/Wheeler Pictures; 22 Louis Requina; 23 (top) Bruce L. Schwartzman; 23 (bottom) National Baseball Library, Cooperstown, New York; 24 Malcolm W. Emmons; 25 (left) AP/Wide World Photos; 25 (right) National Baseball Library, Cooperstown, New York; 26 (left) Bruce L. Schwartzman; 26 (right) Malcolm W. Emmons; 27 (left) Manny Rubio/*Sports Illustrated*; 27 (right) Bruce L. Schwartzman; 28 Patrick Carroll/Photofest; 29 (top) Marvin E. Newman; 29 (bottom) James Drake/*Sports Illustrated*; 30 Bruce L. Schwartzman; 31 Ron Vesely; 32 Ron Menchine Collection/Renée Comet Photography; 33 Brown Brothers; 34 (left) Richard Darcey; 34 (right) AP/Wide World Photos; 35 Focus On Sports, Inc.

The Babe
Pg. 36-37 UPI/Bettmann Newsphotos; 38 (left) AP/Wide World Photos; 38 (right) National Baseball Library, Cooperstown, New York; 39 (left) The Babe Ruth Museum; 39 (right) Culver Pictures; 40 UPI/Bettmann Newsphotos; 41 (top) AP/Wide World Photos; 41 (bottom) The Babe Ruth Museum; 42 UPI/Bettmann Newsphotos; 43 UPI/Bettmann Newsphotos; 44 (left) Courtesy of the Burton Historical Collection of the Detroit Public Library; 44 (right) National Baseball Library, Cooperstown, New York; 45 The Babe Ruth Museum; 46 (left) Ron Menchine Collection/Renée Comet Photography; 46-47 Cleveland Public Library; 48 AP/Wide World Photos; 49 (left) Nickolas Muray, International Museum of Photography at George Eastman House; 49 (right) National Baseball Library, Cooperstown, New York.

How Hard is Hitting?
Pg. 50-51 Neil Leifer/*Sports Illustrated;* 52 (bottom left) AP/Wide World Photos; 52 (top right) Brown Brothers; 53 DiMaggio/Kalish; 54 Malcolm W. Emmons; 55 (left) AP/Wide World Photos; 55 (right) National Baseball Library, Cooperstown, New York; 56 Malcolm W. Emmons; 57 (left) AP/Wide World Photos; 57 (right) Focus On Sports, Inc.; 58 adapted from *Discover* magazine, April 1988; 59 (left) AP/Wide World Photos; 59 (right) Bruce L. Schwartzman; 60 Courtesy of Leaf Inc., Ron Menchine Collection/Renée Comet Photography; 61 AP/Wide World Photos; 62 AP/Wide World Photos; 63 Bruce L. Schwartzman; 64 Photograph © 1989 The Gifted Line, John Grossman, Inc., from the John Grossman Collection of Antique Images; 65 (top left) Culver Pictures; 65 (bottom left) Photoworld/FPG; 65 (right) Hallinan/FPG; 66 (left) T. Tanuma/*Sports Illustrated;* 66 (right) National Baseball Library, Cooperstown, New York; 67 (left) Herb Scharfman/*Sports Illustrated;* 67 (right) Scott Halleran; 68 Bruce L. Schwartzman; 69 (top) Manny Rubio/*Sports Illustrated*; 69 (bottom) Will Hart/ALLSPORT USA; 70 (left) National Baseball Library, Cooperstown, New York; 70 (right) Malcolm W. Emmons; 71 Nancy Hogue; 72 Ron Menchine Collection/Renée Comet Photography; 73 Malcolm W. Emmons; 74 Focus On Sports, Inc.; 75 (top) Neil Leifer/*Sports Illustrated*; 75 (bottom) AP/Wide World Photos.

Power at the Plate
Pg. 76-77 Walter Iooss Jr./*Sports Illustrated*; 78 (left) Jeffrey E. Blackman; 78-79 Jerry Ward/Journalism Services Inc.; 80 (left) Nancy Hogue; 80 (bottom right) Bruce L. Schwartzman; 80-81 (bottom left) Lewis Portnoy/Spectra-Action; 80-81 (top) Jeffrey E. Blackman; 82 (left) John Zimmerman/*Sports Illustrated*; 82 (center) Malcolm W. Emmons; 82-83 Jeffrey E. Blackman; 84 (top) Bruce L. Schwartzman; 84 (bottom) Jeffrey E. Blackman; 85 Walter Iooss Jr./*Sports Illustrated*; 86 (top) Jeffrey E. Blackman; 86 (bottom left) Jeffrey E. Blackman; 86 (bottom right) Nancy Hogue; 87 National Baseball Library, Cooperstown, New York.

The Casey Syndrome
Pg. 88 Jeffrey E. Blackman; 89 Jeffrey E. Blackman; 90 National Baseball Library, Cooperstown, New York; 91 Acme News/*Sports Illustrated*; 92 Jeffrey E. Blackman; 93 Louis Requena; 94 (left) National Baseball Library, Cooperstown, New York; 94 (right) National Baseball Library, Cooperstown, New York; 95 Culver Pictures; 96 Culver Pictures; 97 (bottom left)

Culver Pictures; 97 (top right) Culver Pictures; 97 (bottom right) Culver Pictures; 98 Marvin E. Newman; 99 Tadder/Baltimore; 100 Tony Tomsic; 101 Scott Halleran; 102 Malcolm W. Emmons; 103 Malcolm W. Emmons; 104 Courtesy of © The Topps Company, Inc., Ron Menchine Collection/Renée Comet Photography; 105 AP/Wide World Photos; 106 Fred Kaplan; 107 © 1969 Bob Gomel.

Lumber
Pg. 108-109 Jeffrey E. Blackman; 110 (left) Photograph © 1989 The Gifted Line, John Grossman, Inc., from the John Grossman Collection of Antique Images; 110 (right), 111 (top left), 111 (bottom right), 112 (top left) Hillerich & Bradsby Company Records, University of Louisville Archives, Louisville, Kentucky; 112 (top right) National Baseball Library, Cooperstown New York; 112 (bottom left) Hillerich & Bradsby Company Records, University of Louisville Archives, Louisville, Kentucky; 113 Library of Congress; 114 Library of Congress; 115 © William Strode/Woodfin Camp & Assoc.; 116 Hillerich & Bradsby Company Records, University of Louisville Archives, Louisville, Kentucky; 117 Nancy Hogue; 118-119 National Baseball Library, Cooperstown, New York; 120-121 National Baseball Library, Cooperstown, New York; 122 *The Sporting News*; 123 (left) UPI/Bettmann Newsphotos; 123 (right) AP/Wide World Photos; 124 Thomas Carwile Collection/Renée Comet Photography; 125 (left) © William Strode/Woodfin Camp & Assoc.; 125 (right) © William Strode/Woodfin Camp & Assoc.

Going for the Fences
Pg. 126 Walter Iooss Jr.; 127 AP/Wide World Photos; 128 California Museum of Photography, UC/Riverside; 129 Bruce Davidson/Magnum Photos; 130 Gary Quesada/B. Korab Ltd.; 131 (left) AP/Wide World Photos; 131 (right) Bruce L. Schwartzman; 132-133 Marvin E. Newman; 134 National Baseball Library, Cooperstown, New York, R.J. Mantell Jr.; 135 COMSTOCK INC./Tom Grill; 136 AP/Wide World Photos; 137 Courtesy Minnesota Twins.

Measuring the Man
Pg. 138-139 Ron Menchine Collection/Renée Comet Photography; 140 (left) Brown Brothers; 140 (center) Brown Brothers; 140 (right) AP/Wide World Photos; 141 (left) AP/Wide World Photos; 141 (center) AP/Wide World Photos; 141 (right) UPI/Bettmann Newsphotos; 142 (left) AP/Wide World Photos; 142 (left center) AP/Wide World Photos; 142 (right center) AP/Wide World Photos; 142 (right) AP/Wide World Photos; 143 (left) AP/Wide World Photos; 143 (right) AP/Wide World Photos; 144 (left) Malcolm W. Emmons; 144 (right) AP/Wide World Photos; 145 (left) Culver Pictures; 145 (left center) AP/Wide

World Photos; 145 (right center) Malcolm W. Emmons; 145 (right) Brown Brothers; 146 Culver Pictures; 147 AP/Wide World Photos; 148 DiMaggio/Kalish; 149 Kirk Schlea/ALLSPORT USA; 150 Tadder/Baltimore; 151 DiMaggio/Kalish; 152 Ron Menchine Collection/Renée Comet Photography; 153 AP/Wide World Photos; 154 AP/Wide World Photos; 155 AP/Wide World Photos.

The Power Game
Pg. 156 Bruce L. Schwartzman; 157 Culver Pictures; 158 Cleveland Public Library; 159 National Baseball Library, Cooperstown, New York; 160 National Baseball Library, Cooperstown, New York; 161 (left) Culver Pictures; 161 (right) National Baseball Library, Cooperstown, New York; 162 National Baseball Library, Cooperstown, New York; 163 (top) Gary Quesada/ B. Korab Ltd.; 163 (bottom) Gary Quesada/B. Korab Ltd.; 164 National Baseball Library, Cooperstown, New York; 165 (left) AP/Wide World Photos; 165 (right) AP/Wide World Photos; 166 National Baseball Library, Cooperstown, New York (Don Wingfield Collection); 167 AP/Wide World Photos; 168 National Baseball Library, Cooperstown, New York; 169 (left) AP/Wide World Photos; 169 (right) Photo courtesy of Dr. Lawrence Hogan, Newark Public Library Baseball Archives; 170 Cranston & Elkins/Photofest; 171 UPI/Bettmann Newsphotos; 172 National Baseball Library, Cooperstown, New York; 173 AP/Wide World Photos; 174 Fred Kaplan; 175 National Baseball Library, Cooperstown, New York; 176 Ron Menchine Collection/Renée Comet Photography; 177 (top) © 1961 Robert Riger; 177 (bottom) Malcolm W. Emmons; 178 (top) Malcolm W. Emmons; 178 (bottom) ©1960 Robert Riger; 179 © Robert Riger; 180 (left) Malcolm W. Emmons; 180 (right) Fred Kaplan; 181 (left) H. Peskin/FPG; 181 (right) Fred Kaplan; 182 (left) Bruce L. Schwartzman; 182 (right) Nancy Hogue; 183 Bill Smith/*Sports Illustrated*.

ACKNOWLEDGMENTS

The editors wish to thank:

Thomas Heitz, Patricia Kelly, Peter Clark, Bill Deane, and the staff of the National Baseball Hall of Fame and Museum, Cooperstown, New York; Helen Bowie Campbell and Gregory J. Schwalenberg of the Babe Ruth Museum, Baltimore, Maryland; Bill Williams of Hillerich & Bradsby, Jeffersonville, Indiana; Dave Kelly of the Library of Congress, Washington, D.C.; Steven P. Gietschier of *The Sporting News,* St. Louis, Missouri; Karen Carpenter of *Sports Illustrated,* New York City, New York; Nat Andriani of Wide World Photos, New York City, New York; Sarah Goodyear of Bettman Newsphotos, New York City, New York; Julie Krug of Major League Baseball Productions, New York City, New York; Renee Comet, Washington, D.C.; Sy Berger/The Topps Company, Inc., Brooklyn, New York; Scott Smith of Rawlings Sporting Goods, St. Louis, Missouri; Dr. Sherrill Redmon and David Horvath of the University of Louisville, Louisville, Kentucky; Mary Perencevic of Cleveland Public Library, Cleveland, Ohio; Ellen Hughes of the National Museum of American History, Smithsonian Institution, Washington, D.C.; Kirk Schlea of Allsport Photography USA, San Diego, California; Jo Ann Palmer of Focus on Sports, New York City, New York; Thomas Carwile, Petersburg, Virginia; Jerome Holtzman, Chicago, Illinois; Kathryn J. Phillips, Detroit, Michigan; Thomas Boswell, Washington, D.C.; Barry Codell, Chicago, Illinois; Bob Davids, Washington, D.C.; Woody English, Newark, Ohio; Mark Gallagher, Washington, D.C.; Bill Jenkinson, Willow Grove, Pennsylvania; Lloyd Johnson of SABR, Kansas City, Missouri; Tim Joyce, Washington, D.C.; Ed Kerle, Granville, Ohio; Andy Lewis, Philadelphia, Pennsylvania; Bob McConnell, Wilmington, Delaware; Paul Susman, Chicago, Illinois; the late John Tattersall, Boca Raton, Florida; John Thorn, Saugerties, New York; Paul MacFarlane, St. Louis, Missouri; Dick Cecil, Atlanta, Georgia; Chuck Stevens, Garden Grove, California; Bob Ibach, Chicago, Illinois; Bob Bluthardt, San Angelo, Texas; Robert Boone, Glencoe, Illinois; Eddie Gold, Chicago, Illinois; Gerald Grunska, Glencoe, Illinois; Eugene Murdoch, Williamstown, West Virginia; Edgar "Pete" Palmer, Lexington, Massachusetts; Yoichi Nagata, Kawasaki, Japan.

World of Baseball is produced and published by Redefinition, Inc.

WORLD OF BASEBALL

Editor	Glen B. Ruh
Design Director	Robert Barkin
Production Director	Irv Garfield
Associate Editor	Larry Moffi
Picture Research	Rebecca Hirsh, Louis P. Plummer, Catherine M. Chase
Designer	Ruth Burke
Senior Writer	Jonathan Kronstadt
Editorial Research	Ed Dixon, Victoria Salin
Writers	Robert Kiener, Gerald Jonas
Editorial Assistants	Elizabeth D. McLean, Janet Pooley
Design Assistants	Randy Cook, Collette Conconi
Illustration	Dale Glasgow
Production Assistant	Kimberly Fornshill
Copy Preparation	Gail Cerra
Index	Lynne Hobbs

REDEFINITION

Administration	Margaret M. Higgins, June M. Nolan
Fulfillment Manager	Karen L. DeLisser
Marketing Director	Harry Sailer
Finance Director	Vaughn A. Meglan
PRESIDENT	Edward Brash

Library of Congress Cataloging-in-Publication Data
The sluggers/John Holway
   (World of Baseball)
   Includes index.
   1. Baseball–United States–History
I.Title II.Series
GV869.H55 1989   88–064026
796.357'09273 B
ISBN 0–924588–00–4

Printed in U.S.A.
10 9 8 7 6 5 4 3 2

CONTRIBUTORS

John Holway is a prolific baseball writer, a long-time member of the Society for American Baseball Research, and a frequent contributor to *Baseball Research Journal* and *The National Pastime*. His books include *Voices from the Great Black Baseball Leagues, Black Baseball Stars,* and (with John Thorn) *The Pitchers.*

Henry Staat is Series Consultant for World of Baseball. A member of the Society for American Baseball Research since 1982, he helped initiate the concept for the series. He is an editor with Wadsworth, Inc., a publisher of college textbooks.

Ron Menchine, an advisor and special sports collector, shared baseball materials he has been collecting for 40 years. A sportscaster and sports director for numerous radio stations, he announced the last three seasons played by the Senators in Washington, D.C. He currently freelances on radio and television and has had roles in two motion pictures.

This book is one of a series that celebrates America's national pastime.

Redefinition also offers a World of Baseball Top Ten Stat Finder.

For subscription information and prices please write:
  Customer Service, Redefinition, Inc., P.O. Box 25336, Alexandria, Virginia 22313

The text of this book is set in Century Old Style; display type is Helvetica and Gill Sans. The paper is 70 pound Warrenflo Gloss supplied by Stanford Paper Company. Typesetting by Darby Graphics, Alexandria, Virginia. Color separation by Colotone, Inc., North Branford, Connecticut. Printed and bound by Ringier America, New Berlin, Wisconsin.